B
Bus

W9-CFI-532

A

GEORGE BUSH
MAN OF
INTEGRITY

GEORGE BUSH MAN OF INTEGRITY

WITH
DOUG WEAD

HARVEST HOUSE PUBLISHERS
Eugene, Oregon 97402

Back cover photo: Dave Valdez, The White House

1st Printing — February 1988

MAN OF INTEGRITY

Copyright © 1988 by Harvest House Publishers
Eugene, Oregon 97402

Library of Congress Catalog Card Number 87-083229
Trade edition ISBN 0-89081-667-0
Cloth edition ISBN 0-89081-652-2

Printed in the United States of America.

To Barbara
A Lover of Books

Acknowledgments

Special thanks to the Vice President and his family
and a long list of staff members who made this project
possible—

Craig Fuller
Lee Atwater
David Bates
David Valdez
Patty Presock
Debra Romash
Jan Bermeister
Don Iloff
Cathleen Pollard

Thanks to Bob Hawkins, Sr., Eileen Mason, and all
the wonderful people at Harvest House.

And a warm thanks to Rich Bond who one afternoon
said "Sounds like a good idea; go ahead," and thus
launched the whole project.

---

*Royalty proceeds from the sale of this book are being
donated on behalf of The Washington Charity Dinner
to City-Schools, Inc., an effective private public program dealing with school dropouts.*

Contents

A Letter to a Grandson

Dear "P",

I've been thinking a lot about this summer. I had a very good time; it was fun going out in the Fidelity. *Remember the day we caught all those greasy pollock? That was a good day.*

You and Noelle liked the beach a lot, but I don't like going there. Now I am too old for that. If I get cold I get stiff, just like my own dad used to. This year for the first time I felt a little that way.

Another thing that was fun for me, but wasn't too much fun for you and Noelle, was when we went over to see my mother—"Ganny" to your Dad and Mom, "Great Ganny" to you. I loved checking up on her—wasn't she nice? She always cares how the other guy feels.

But "P", I've been thinking about it a lot—the most fun was the big rock boat, climbing out on it, watching you and Noelle playing on it. Near the end of the summer, when the moon was full and the tides were higher, there was that special day at high tide when it almost seemed like the boat was real.

I think the most fun was that rock boat. . . . Maybe it's 'cause just at that moment I turned a corner in my life. I could see down the road with no fear and I suddenly had great happiness because I felt that in 50 years or so you'd be there, out on that rock boat, loving the ocean as I do, surrounded by family love and aching a little when it gets cold.

I can't wait till next summer!

> *Love,*
> *Gamby*

A letter from the Vice President
to his grandson George Prescott Bush.

GEORGE BUSH
MAN OF
INTEGRITY

- 1 -
Shot Down over the Pacific

My first interview with the Vice President was held in the late winter of 1982, in his office at the West Wing of the White House.

The Vice President's Press Secretary, Pete Teeley, had sat through hundreds of these interviews, so I thought it would be a good idea to get some advice from him. Why waste time rehashing stories already on the public record? Those I could find.

Teeley suggested that the great untold story of George Bush was his war record. When the Bush-for-President bandwagon was at full speed in 1980, his war record had received a prominent place in the official biography. But though it was often mentioned, the accounts never included many details.

It was a couple of years later, while updating the George Bush biography, that Pete Teeley had stumbled across the Navy's Citation of Bravery. Teeley was surprised when he learned the extent of the heroics of the young George Bush, but he was not surprised at how unassuming the Vice President had been about his World War II record.

The reluctance to boast of personal achievements is one of the more pronounced and famous characteristics of the complex George Bush personality. While it was endearing to find someone who had achieved so much while still remaining relatively unaffected by it all, friends and advisors found that there were times when this trait could be quite frustrating. Political consultants were especially antsy when the

1

Vice President refused to step forward and take credit for something that was clearly his.

The key, Teeley assured me, was to come prepared. So I armed myself with what little material already existed on the subject and a determination that I would obtain George Bush's firsthand account of the day he was shot down in the Pacific during World War II.

Actually, it turned out to be one of the best interviews I was to have with George Bush. The Vice President's Press Secretary, who had alerted me to the whole idea, had also been telling the Vice President that he needed to open up and get his story on the record. So perhaps the timing was right.

When the interview started, we were alone. But then at some midway point a staffer appeared at the door giving the customary prearranged signal, "I'm sorry, Mr. Vice President, but you have to go." This really meant, of course, that *I* had to go. But evidently this afternoon the Vice President's schedule had more flexibility. He waved away the interruption and our interview continued.

By the time we were finished, several staffers and secretaries had joined us, at first standing and then (at the Vice President's insistence) sitting on the various couches and chairs. For a short time business came to a stop.

With the fireplace popping and whistling, the Vice President gave one of the best accounts of his dangerous missions as America's youngest Navy pilot.

"The sun shone intermittently through a broken cloud cover as our aircraft carrier, the *San Jacinto*, steamed toward Chichi Jima, a little island south of Japan. It was September 2, 1944, and as I strapped myself into my aircraft (a torpedo bomber called an Avenger), I thought to myself that this would be a bad day to be shot down.

"We were supposed to knock out some radio stations on Chichi Jima. It was all part of a plan to interrupt Japanese communications in preparation for an invasion of the Palau Islands.

"We had tried to finish the job the day before, but hadn't been successful. The island was very well-defended. I think our squadron lost one plane.

"I was part of the VT51 squadron. We had 34 planes assigned to the carrier. We really had a very vulnerable ship, light and thin-skinned. It had been rushed into service. Of course that gave it an advantage, too; it was fast, and as a result we saw a lot of action.

"The Avenger would take a crew of three. I was the pilot up front; behind me was my rear gunner, Leo Nadeau; and underneath, with a machine gun, was the radioman, John Delaney. The rear gunner, Leo Nadeau, didn't go that morning. It saved his life.

"The three of us had seen a lot of action before September second. That spring my roommate had been shot down. The war in the Pacific was really reaching its peak; the enemy was up against the wall and they were tough. I remember making a forced landing in the middle of the ocean, with the three of us barely getting away before the plane exploded.

"There was an accident on board the *San Jacinto* in which a pilot's leg was thrown across the deck. It landed right in front of me, quivering. We were all stunned—here was this body cut in two—and then one of the officers came along and yelled, 'Get this mess cleaned up!' So everybody went back to work."

Why did your crew suddenly change that morning?

"Ted White came up to me and asked if he could go along as gunner. He was an old friend of the family, a Yale graduate. His parents had always wanted him to be a pilot.

"It was obvious that it was going to be a pretty dangerous raid. I told him we had picked up some pretty serious antiaircraft fire the day before, but if it was okay with the commander it was okay with me. Well, he was pretty excited. It was going to be his first raid."

He was killed?

"He never came back.

"We were the second plane in, so they were ready for us. It was called glide-bombing, which is different from a dive-bomber, which puts the flaps on and drops at about 60 degrees. We were coming in at about 30 degrees, but the feel in a torpedo bomber gave the sensation of going straight down."

Do you remember the exact moment when you were hit?

"I'll never forget it.

"There were black explosions all around us and then a flash of light. The plane was lifted forward and we were suddenly enveloped in flames.

"I remember looking out and seeing the flames running along the wing where the fuel tanks were and where the wings fold. I thought, '*This is really bad.*' The cockpit was filled with smoke, so it was difficult to read the instruments, but we were falling fast. I pulled out of the dive, finished the run, and then turned back out over the water."

The official records say that in spite of damage to your own plane, you continued your dive and scored hits on the radio station. The report talks about complete disregard for your own safety and about courage to press the attack even after your own plane was engulfed in flames and smoke.

"It was an instinct—there really wasn't much time to think about it. Everyone who went into combat was brave."

But everyone didn't win the Distinguished Flying Cross medal.

"To tell you the truth, I thought I was a goner. I looked

back and saw that my rear gunner was out. He had been machine-gunned to death right where he was.

"So then I turned back over the water and we bailed out."

But Delaney was killed too, and you were the only survivor.

"He was evidently cut to ribbons as he parachuted down. I was luckier. Trying to get out in a hurry, I ended up banging my head on the plane and my chute got caught on the tail and then broke free, but I got out. My rubber raft had broken free, so I swam over and climbed in."

The story is that the Japanese were shooting from the shore, and they were coming after you in their own boats.

"I'm told that some of the fellows circled back and strafed the enemy boats and that's what saved me.

"Chichi Jima was part of the Bonin Islands, and after the war I found out that the enemy soldiers on those islands were pretty fierce warriors. Among other things, a war crimes tribunal found them guilty of torturing and beheading downed airmen. There were even some pretty extraordinary stories of cannibalism. Of course if I had known that, I would have paddled all the way to Hawaii."

So much time has passed since World War II. The horror seems to have gone out of it. There have even been television sitcoms on the subject.

"There has been time for healing. The West Germans and Japanese are two of our most important allies, even though sometimes we are passionate economic rivals.

"But I can assure you that there is no such thing as a funny war. They are all terrible and tragic events, chewing up hundreds of thousands of young people even before they have had a chance to live, and leaving behind broken-hearted families.

"I can tell you this: If I'm ever in the position to call the shots, I'm not going to rush to send somebody else's kids into a war. I know what it was like to be a 21-year-old kid out there in the middle of the Pacific Ocean, disoriented, nauseous, agonizing over the deaths of my closest friends, and terrorized by the thought of imminent capture.

"To some people war may appear glamorous and romantic in the history books, and it is tragic that each generation usually experiences several wars until it has had its fill of them.

"I suppose that's why I feel so strongly about maintaining a powerful defense—so that this country never has to go to war again."

So you were shot down in the middle of the Pacific Ocean . . .

"I had injured myself trying to get out of that plane before it crashed. It really wasn't a serious injury, but just a strawberry—the kind you get from sliding into home plate. But some of the pilots circling overhead saw the blood all over my face and thought the worst.

"They dropped some medicine from the air and I paddled over and picked it up. I checked myself out to see if I was okay. There wasn't much time. The frustrating thing was that the wind was blowing me back toward the beach, so I had to keep paddling to stay out.

"I remember the drone of our planes disappearing and wondering what was going to happen to me. Of course, I prayed. I thought 'This is it—it's all over.'

"I was out there paddling for a couple of hours, with the wind blowing me back toward shore, when this submarine rose up out of the waters. It was like an apparition. At first I thought, 'Maybe I'm delirious,' and then, when I concluded that it was a submarine all right, I feared that it

George Bush graduates from Phillips Academy, Andover, Massachusetts, in June 1942. On June 12, his 18th birthday, he enlists in the U.S. Navy Reserve as a Seaman Second Class.

Receiving his wings and commission while still 18, George Bush becomes the youngest pilot in the U.S. Navy.

might be Japanese. It just seemed to me too lucky and too farfetched that it would be an American submarine. But then I saw the American sailors running back and forth across the deck and I knew I was going to make it—that for some reason I was going to live through this thing."

How long were you on board the submarine?

"As it turned out, they had just begun a pretty dangerous mission in enemy waters. There wasn't anything they could do with me but take me along. So I spent the next 30 days on a U.S. submarine.

"I can tell you that there were some times when I wasn't so sure whether I had been rescued or not. It was a frightening experience, and the longer it lasted the more I grew to respect those men.

"We used to argue over which career was the most dangerous. They would say that they never wanted to be a pilot because you were too vulnerable as a pilot, and if you got hit, it was all over. Yet here I was, living proof that you could fall out of the sky and live to talk about it.

"I would tell them that this was going to be the last submarine duty I ever did. Sometimes there were depth charges exploding all around us. If there had been just a hairline crack in the skin of that submarine, it would have been all over. Where are you going to go when you're already under the surface of the ocean?

"Of course, with my being on board that long, they gave me something to do. In those close quarters everybody pitched in. It was an experience I will never forget—firing torpedoes at the enemy and then hiding right under their noses for days on end. Our skipper was eventually given the Silver Star for the amount of tonnage he sank. When the patrol was over, I was given a brief rest at Pearl Harbor and then sent back out to the fleet again. I'm still waiting for my bonus check from the U.S. Navy for submarine service!"

You must have had some sense of destiny about all of this. Your co-pilot and gunner were dead, and you were very lucky to have gotten out of it alive.

"Oh, yes, there was all of that. People talk about a kind of foxhole Christianity, where you're in trouble and think you're going to die, and so you want to make everything right with God and everybody else right there in the last minute.

"But this was just the opposite of that. I had already faced death, and God had spared me. I had this very deep and profound gratitude and a sense of wonder. Sometimes when there is disaster people will pray, 'Why me?' In an opposite way I had the same question: Why had I been spared and what did God have for me?

"At night when we would surface, I used to enjoy my time on the watch. It was absolutely dark in the middle of the Pacific; the nights were so clear and the stars so brilliant. It was wonderful and energizing, a time to talk to God.

"One of the things I realized out there all alone was how much family meant to me. Having faced death and been given another chance to live, I could see just how important those values and principles were that my parents had instilled in me, and of course how much I loved Barbara, the girl I knew I would marry. Her name had been painted on my plane."

Were you a dreamer as a young man? Did you have goals to do great things?

"I suppose, like all young men, I was a dreamer. But I never did set up a grand design for my life. I've always believed that you must do well in whatever it is that you do, and in that sense I set objectives along the way and then tried to attain them. For example, I had wanted to go right into the Navy when the war broke out. But my parents and relatives were upset; they felt that the thing for me to do was go on to college. Yet I was shaken by what had happened at Pearl Harbor, and I was patriotic and wanted to do something about it. So I dug in my heels and pulled it off. I won my wings and commission at the age of 18, at the time the youngest pilot in the United States Navy. I was determined to see combat and then after the war get into college, and so I did. I've always been one to concentrate on what's at hand."

There is no unique George Bush philosophy of success?

"If there is, it's not systematic. I just say, Do your best, stand for something, accomplish something, be a doer and not a critic. If you don't like things, get in and try to change them. If you've been lucky enough to take something out of the system, put something back into it.

"My family instilled some concepts in me at a very early age. They believed very strongly in Christian ethics, kindness and helping others, and I've embraced that for myself.

"In 1980, when I started running for the Presidency, some of the most knowledgeable and talented people warned me, 'You're just going to get hurt.'

"In a sense they may have been right. Perhaps there was no chance in 1980, but we worked hard, raised money, and paid all our bills. We had an incredible experience with hundreds of thousands of people supporting us. If I had waited around for somebody else to tell me to do this, I wouldn't be sitting here talking to you now.

"Give life everything you've got: Don't hold back and don't look for the easy way out; just go ahead and do what you should do."

You were still in the Navy when you married Barbara?

"Yes, I was in some pretty heavy action over the Philippines when I got Christmas leave. It was an unforgettably happy time for me during Christmas of 1944. "But the war was still on. If you had said that it would all be over within six months, no one would have believed you. It's true that the Germans were falling back on the eastern front, but the Battle of the Bulge had been launched, and all these American boys were getting chewed up. And in the Pacific theater it looked like we were only at the halfway mark, with a long war of costly island-hopping ahead of us.

"Yet with all that tragedy as a backdrop, here I was back in Connecticut again with family and friends, and at Christmas on top of that. So Barbara and I were married, and for me it's been one of the world's greatest love stories ever since."

Do you remember where you were when the war ended?

"I'll never forget it. We were in Virginia Beach, Virginia, anticipating reassignment back to combat at any moment. The war in the Pacific still seemed like it was going to stretch on forever. Ten of the 14 original pilots in our squad had already been killed. I had to live with the prospect that if I were to get shot down this time, it might mean leaving behind a beautiful young widow.

"And then Truman dropped the bombs. A few days later the war was over and there was an unbelievable celebration. On the base, pilots were running out into the streets and hugging each other. People everywhere were crying and laughing.

"Barbara and I slipped away to a little chapel. I remember thinking about all my buddies who had died, and I remember squeezing Barbara's hand and thanking God one more time for letting me live to see this day of peace."

- 2 -
Prosperity with a Purpose

In the spring of 1986 some days were better than others for Vice President George Bush. So I was pretty happy when I caught up with him on a good day. For starters, his two favorite baseball teams, the Houston Astros and the New York Mets, were leading in their respective divisions of the National League. For an even more important piece of good news, a new *Washington Post*-ABC poll showed him trouncing his prospective rivals as the favorite for the Republican nomination in '88.

Early that morning I shared a taxi to Andrews Air Force Base with Ron Kaufman, a longtime Bush political strategist and a good friend of mine. When the Vice President had decided to start up a political action committee, he had tapped Ron to get things going. Kaufman and I listened to our taxi driver's cogent analysis of what Congress was up to and what it would eventually settle on. I couldn't help wondering why none of the television networks had ever brought on a couchful of Washington cabbies to give their views and liven up those Sunday afternoon news talk shows!

We cleared security at the distinguished visitors' lounge before walking out the back gate toward Air Force Two. The two 727's which constituted the equipment then available for the Vice President stood side by side about a hundred yards away. On the long march out across the tarmac we had a chance to take them both in. They were big white birds, with blue and gold stripes running across their sides and the stars and stripes displayed on their tails. The words "UNITED STATES OF AMERICA" were stamped with understated elegance along the length of the jets. Uniformed Air Force guards, at full attention, stood stiffly at the steps.

For the chronic traveler, the most wonderful thing about Air Force Two is to find yourself on a plane full of friends as opposed to strangers. Politicos, journalists, and the Vice President's family visit freely. The stewards and stewardesses actually smile, and even the Secret Service agents relax a little. Of course, all the seats are first-class, and the Vice President and Barbara are so unimposing that no one is made to feel less important than anyone else.

The jet was still on a steep climb when George Bush's popular personal aide, Tim McBride, stepped back to my seat. "Doug, the Vice President would like to see you up front."

George Bush was seated comfortably at his desk. He was wearing his blue Vice Presidential flight jacket and munching on grapes out of a fruit bowl. His new Press Secretary, Marlin Fitzwater, sat on a couch opposite us, balancing himself and leaning in from time to time as he tried to hear above the roar of the engines. On one side of the front cabin wall was a full-color picture of the compound at Kennebunkport, Maine. On the other side was the Burton Parish at Williamsburg, Virginia.

Malcolm Baldridge, the Secretary of Commerce, was also in the front cabin. The Bush-Baldridge friendship was an old one. The Vice President reportedly liked Baldridge's style. The Secretary was a quiet, effective administrator who usually understated his case. Only a year later he would be injured in a rodeo and die from the accident. I'll never forget that scene on Air Force Two, with the Secretary quietly reading as he sat next to the Vice President's son, Marvin Bush. I was thinking what a great combination the Bush-Baldridge team would be if George Bush became President. But none of us on the jet that day knew the tragedy that lay ahead for the Secretary of Commerce. It was a happy time, and the Vice President started out talking baseball.

"Some of my best friends are in baseball—Joe Morgan, Nolan Ryan, Rusty Staub. I guess you can tell I'm an Astros fan! Some of the new kids are doing pretty well for us this year, but I'm patient and loyal even when we're losing."

Do you still get to see many games?

"Not too many. When I can, I go to the All-Star game or maybe take in the World Series. A couple of years ago I called up Carl Yastrzemski. It was just an idea, but he joined me for the All-Star game. We had a marvelous time.

"I've always liked competitive athletics. I like the influence that sports has had on my life and on my children. I'm convinced that sports teaches us a lot.

"When you open up a newspaper you usually see lots of stories of pain. By necessity newspapers are basically a chronicle of the world's problems, its floods and wars and scandals. Even the financial page can be like that. But the sports section is always an account of personal achievement."

I've heard that the New York Mets are also a favorite team of yours.

"That goes back to my U.N. days in New York. Sometimes we would take foreign visitors to see a little piece of 'Americana.' Also, I had an uncle who was part owner of the Mets. So I've watched them very closely, especially in the early days. It was great fun."

You had quite a baseball career yourself as captain of the Yale team.

"My batting average was too low, but I had some great times at Yale!

"We had an excellent coach in Ethan Allen, a former major leaguer. We won the Eastern Intercollegiate Championship all three years, competing with some of the nation's toughest teams. And in 1947 we went to Kalamazoo, Michigan, for the first Collegiate World Series, which we lost to California. In 1948 we were right back in the World Series again, this time getting edged out by Southern California in the last game.

"One of the stars on our team was our ace pitcher, Frank Quinn. He signed with the Boston Red Sox for 100,000 dollars. In those days it was an astronomical amount of money for a college-age baseball player. Another pitcher, Dick Monville, signed with the Pittsburgh Pirates. As a matter of fact, there may have been six out of our starting nine who ended up in the majors.

"When it came to sports, Yale didn't usually get much respect, so it was exciting for the university to produce a winner. We had a groundskeeper named Morris Greenberg, who kept the stadium playing field immaculate. Everyone took pride in the team."

Babe Ruth was a childhood idol of yours?

"Actually I was probably more of a Lou Gehrig fan. When I was a boy my father often took me to Yankee Stadium, and I would dream of playing first base someday. But one day, years later, Babe Ruth paid a visit to Yale University. He came to present his papers. So we held a ceremony at the stadium. Since I was captain of the team, I had the privilege of receiving his papers in behalf of Yale. It was a great thrill.

"By that time Babe was wasting away with cancer. It was hard to realize that he had been one of America's most gifted athletes. It was one of the greatest days of my young life to meet him."

Was there ever some special time—a home run, a close fielding play?

"Actually, about the only home run I ever hit came at a perfect time. It was our game with the Yale alumni. These guys were really trying to show us up. To make things even more interesting, my young uncle was pitching for the alumni. He would never forget it, and neither will I. He was determined to strike me out and I was determined to at least connect. Well, I connected all right, sending the ball into the left-field stands. It was a pleasure that sustained me all during my youth, and in a sense even now in my adult years."

A lot has been said about your family—your father's great success, the wealth and privilege. After graduating from Yale you had it made. The story is that you could have stayed back East with the family in a permanent job with Brown Brothers Harriman, but that you rejected all of that to head out to Texas.

"I wanted to get out on my own and do something for myself. It was kind of that call, 'Go West, young man, go West.' Like a lot of Navy couples, Barbara and I had been transferred all over the place, and both of us had loved Texas. We had vowed that one day we would go back. My uncle told me about an opening for work in the oil fields. So we packed everything in our red Studebaker and headed West."

Is it true that your first job was pushing a broom?

"Yes, that's true. I started out as a clerk in an oil equipment company in Odessa. Barbara and I lived in a humble little apartment, and we shared the bathroom with a lady who lived in a house trailer next to us.

"Sometimes I pushed a broom—whatever needed to be done. Pretty soon they had me selling. I was all over the place—Muleshoe, Pecos. Eventually Barbara and I were making enough money to buy a house in Midland.

"It was an exciting time to live in West Texas. All kinds of people were striking it rich in oil. The boom was on, and I suppose it was only natural that we would be bitten by the bug ourselves. Eventually my neighbor John Overbey and I launched our own company. The idea was to take a chance by buying up the available mineral rights from the farmers and then try to broker them to bigger companies. It was a very risky business, and we considered ourselves lucky to have survived.

"A few years later we merged with Hugh and Bill Liedtke to form Zapata Petroleum. The Liedtke brothers were true business talents, and of course they went on to found Pennzoil and other enterprises."

Were there setbacks, times when you thought you had lost it all?

"That's the very nature of the oil business. Sometimes we had nothing in the bank but opportunity. It was a tough business and still is, but a lot of very hard work was done to improve our chances.

"Eventually we split with the Liedtkes. They took the land oil business and I moved to Houston to take over our offshore operation. Offshore oil was something new. As a matter of fact, we built the world's first offshore drilling platforms. They were mammoth undertakings. Imagine concrete-and-steel islands in the ocean!

"Yes, there were setbacks. One time we got word of a hurricane in the Gulf. We got our men off the platforms, and the next day I took out a search helicopter. When I reached the area there was nothing there. I flew for hours and hours, but I had this feeling in my stomach that I

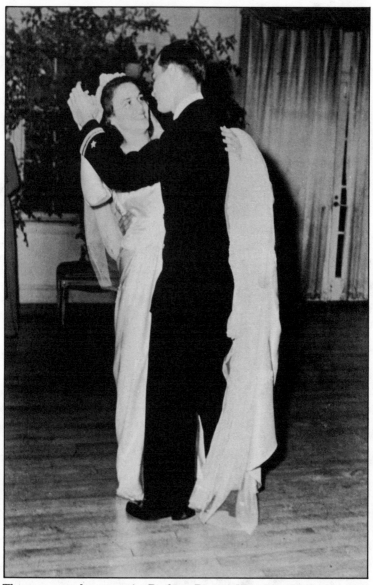

The young war hero marries Barbara Pierce of Rye, New York, daughter of the publisher of *McCall's* magazine, on January 6, 1945.

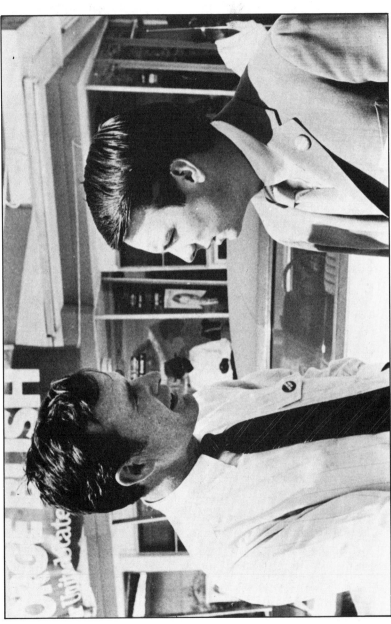

George Bush campaigning for the U.S. Congress. He was one of only two Republicans elected to Congress from Texas in 1966.

wouldn't find anything. Sure enough, the whole platform had been washed away. It represented a big piece of our business, but there was nothing we could do but pick up where we left off and carry on."

Meanwhile, back in Connecticut, your father, Prescott Bush, was elected to the United States Senate.

"My parents told us to always give something back. We had all worked hard and achieved our own individual success, but that was not enough. There was this philosophy of service. Life had been good to us, and we owed society something."

Your own political career was launched in Houston?

"Actually Barbara and I got involved before then. In 1952 we helped organize the first Republican Primary ever held in Midland, Texas. We'll never forget it. At the end of the day we counted the votes—mine, Barbara's, and one Democrat's!

"Back then we could have had a Southern Republican Leadership conference in two booths at a pancake house. In fact, we did!

"Barbara and I laugh about it now. It's inspiring to travel throughout the South today and see these huge crowds of Republicans, but I can tell you it wasn't easy. We know how hard the Party regulars worked. Rambo and Rocky may be tough, but Rambo never had to knock on doors of fifth-generation Democrats and tell them why they ought to switch to being Republicans.

"But now they're switching in record numbers. In fact, when I speak to Republican audiences in the South I'll often take an informal survey and ask who used to be registered Democrats. I'll say, 'Please stand up.' When they did that at the White House, one fellow popped out of his seat right away—Ronald Reagan!

"When we moved to Houston, I went down to the local Republican headquarters and joined right in. A few years later, in 1963, some of my friends encouraged me to run for Harris County Chairman, which I won. So my little political career had begun. The next year I ran for the United States Senate, and of course I didn't make it."

Yet in many ways it was a success for you. People considered it a pretty gutsy thing to do, and it was certainly a turning point in your political career.

"I considered myself a Goldwater Republican. I went to the National Convention as a part of the Texas Delegation and cast my vote for Barry Goldwater like everyone else. But we all got buried in the Johnson landslide.

"This wasn't exactly a success in itself. If I had quit politics right then, people would have viewed it as a failure. But it was a good campaign and a lot of people had worked very hard. We ran ahead of Goldwater by 200,000 votes and polled more votes than any Republican had ever won in the state's history. That gained me some national recognition.

"The only reason it wasn't a worse defeat was because I didn't quit. Instead, I used my defeat as a springboard for my campaign for the United States Congress. I sold my stock in the oil business and really committed myself to the contest. Two years later I was elected as one of only two Republican Congressmen from the State of Texas. Sometimes how we react to a problem or a defeat is as important as the problem itself."

In the 1960's and 70's politicians were all neatly categorized. There was a great polarization: conservative-liberal. Yet to many people you were an elusive quality.

"By most definitions I was considered conservative, and still am. If I remember correctly, in 1967, after serving a year in Congress, the conservative groups rated me pretty high. I subscribe to the theory 'That government governs best that governs least.' As a businessman I saw the trouble and frustrations with an overregulated marketplace. It was counterproductive and seemed to hurt the very people the government was most wanting to help.

"My controversy with some of the ultraconservatives stemmed from a vote on the open-housing issue. From a political standpoint, there was no choice. I represented the 7th Congressional District, Houston. Most of these voters had a piece of the American dream. They didn't want Hispanics and Blacks and other minorities moving in on them. But it seemed to me that a truly 'conservative' interpretation of the Constitution guaranteed the rights of all Americans. If doing the right thing meant being a one-term Congressman, that was all right with me.

"So we had this big meeting back in Houston, and I got booed and jeered. Yet when it was over they gave me a standing ovation. Even if many people didn't understand my rationale, they did understand that I was acting out of principle.

"The South is much different today. The neoconservatives are very interested in leading the way to meet the needs of minorities. Conservative think tanks are churning out new ideas. Today you won't find any conservative leaders who would vote differently than I did then, and no conservatives are out there saying, 'Let's repeal open housing.' "

Do you think the Republicans will ever win back the Black voters?

"I hope so. We have some good Republican Black leaders emerging. It would be a good thing for the Blacks as well as for the Republican Party. Blacks have been exploited and taken for granted by the Democrats, just as they once were in the Republican Party. That's the danger of being a one-party minority. The Blacks would be wise to have more of their advocates in both parties.

"The Republicans are reaching out with ideas and concepts that can work with little risk, since they won't compromise programs already in place, but many Black political leaders are already so committed in their own personal careers as Democrats that they find it hard to promote a Republican idea, even if it's a good one."

Mr. Vice President, several years ago a group of former writers with the John Birch Society began issuing pamphlets about the Trilateral Commission. The charge was that the Council on Foreign Relations and then later the Trilateral Commission were in fact conspiracies to form a "one-world government." They proposed that the Commission secretly ran things, pulling the strings in Moscow as well as Washington. Now all this literature is recycling. The more sensational the accusations, the more popular the appeal. How do you respond to all this? They name you and almost everybody else of prominence as part of it all.

"As I understood it, the Trilateral Commission was founded in 1973 because of a fear of some people that the U.S. State Department was pursuing a dangerous policy of building relationships with our adversaries, Russia and China, while neglecting our 'laterals'—Canada, Japan, and our allies in Western Europe.

"I resigned from both organizations in 1978 after being a member less than two years, but I didn't resign for any sinister reason. Both the Trilateral Commission and the Council on Foreign Relations published their membership. They were not secret organizations.

"As a matter of fact, we were told that Ronald Reagan and I were the only candidates running for President in 1980 who were not members.

"The Commission took no stand on any issue. Its membership included such patriotic and outstanding Republicans as Bill Brock, former Ambassador Anne Armstrong, and Senator Bill Roth of Delaware, co-author of the income-tax-slashing Kemp-Roth Bill."

I understand that some of these publications are now attacking President Reagan because the White House hosted the Commission in 1984. Here is the greatest conservative leader in recent times and a great President. You know that must hurt him.

"To say that anyone who was ever associated with the Trilateral Commission or the Council on Foreign Relations is a conspirator against the United States or is traitorous is just absurd. I risked my life fighting for our country during World War II. I have never belonged to, and would never belong to, any organization that had devious designs upon America or that favored one-world government.

"There are people in this country who will always look for conspiratorial explanations for the problems we face. If oil and gas prices go up, it's a conspiracy by the energy companies. If we blunder in foreign policy, it's a conspiracy by international bankers. In reality our problems are due to our own mistakes, and sometimes they are only random manifestations of a free marketplace."

How do you deal with the pain of politics—the betrayals, the exploiters, the crassness of some of the media attacks? I've sometimes wondered how Lyndon Johnson or Jimmy Carter endured rejection from the very groups of people they championed.

"You have to stick with the principles and values you were taught. That's what sustains you.

"Carl Shurz once said something to the effect that ideals are like stars: We may never reach them, but like those old mariners on the troubled seas, we chart our course by them. With them we reach our destiny. No matter how stormy the waters sometimes look, you have to stick to your ideals."

It's interesting that Ronald Reagan is sometimes called the "Teflon President" because negative just doesn't stick to him. Your career is not only varied but it sometimes seems to have a sheen of that Teflon coating all its own. After serving at the U.N. you were appointed Chairman of the Republican National Committee. You ran it right during the middle of Watergate and yet you came through unscathed, with both your reputation for being loyal and your integrity intact.

"You can make decisions that people don't like without incurring their wrath. Often *how* you do something is more meaningful than *what* you do.

"To achieve something in this world, you've got to be willing to take risks. That's where my critics end up confused about me. I don't fit neatly into their mold.

"I should have gone to college at 18, but I joined the Navy; I should have stayed back East and worked my father's prosperous business, but I went West and started out on my own. I'm convinced that you can't just sit around waiting for things to happen. You've got to take the chance, go after it, take the tough assignment.

"President Ford offered me an ambassadorship to England or France—pretty glamorous duty. I opted for China. Advisors warned me against going to the CIA; it was supposed to be a political dead end. It was the worst time to go over to the agency, but I grew from the experience."

Let me ask you about style. Gerald Ford described you as "unselfish." Your family legend carries with it the nickname George "have-half" Bush. Your mother says you were always opening up the kitchen to neighborhood friends, offering your food: "Here, have half." Is there anything to that?

"The term 'unselfish' is very broad. I would like to be known as a team player. Are you always looking out for your own neck? Are you always positioning yourself? Are you always thinking about what's best for you?

"You can't be an effective or good Vice President unless you're a team player. Some people are cynical about a Vice President's role; they call it 'buttering up.' But I don't believe that. I believe that it's highly responsible to work in a complementary way with your Chief Executive."

You've been a strong Vice President. You've been brought right into the decision-making process in the West Wing of the White House. But unlike your predecessor, Walter Mondale, you have managed to remain very low-key. Is that calculated?

"No, it's not calculated; it's natural. It's back to my philosophy of being a team player."

But earlier you suggested that to be successful you must take risks and be bold.

"There's no contradiction here. There was a great political risk in going to the CIA at the time, but to me that risk had to be sublimated because of what could be done for the country. That's what I mean by boldness. I don't mean seeking confrontation or having to spill every iota of inner feeling to attract attention, or to lash out against an idea when doing so conflicts with the overall good of the administration. We're talking about apples and oranges."

I'm thinking now about the assassination attempt. Time

magazine captured it well in a quote. They said you were firm without being pushy.
Everybody talked about the cabinet meeting where you refused to sit in the chairman's seat while the President was recovering in the hospital. You simply left the President's chair empty. It was a great symbolic gesture, and it was revealing.

"That was just an instinctive action; it wasn't calculated."

———————

At still another time and another place on the road, the subject of the Vice President's early years in business came up again. He talked about what he had learned regarding people and their motivations. The Wall Street scandal was big news.

———————

"Some of those people in West Texas would rather have starved to death than cheat anybody.

"We need a revival of traditional ethical standards. Despite our national prosperity, many Americans are concerned that we have strayed from our fundamental values.

"It really is disturbing when those in privileged positions fail to uphold the trust that is placed in them. Public service has been hurt by individuals who lack the judgment or character to put the public's business above their own self-interest. And it's as big a problem on Wall Street as it is in Washington. Those of us in leadership positions in government, and in all walks of life, must make something very clear: Unethical behavior will not be tolerated!

"What would the Democrats do about this? Regulate, regulate, regulate. Of course wrongdoing should be punished, and hard. But more red tape is not the answer. You can't legislate ethical behavior. But you can lead by example. I want people who want to make a contribution, not to make a buck. You can be sure of this: A Bush administration will be known for its integrity."

Some people have characterized this as the era of greed.

"That's sad.

"Jobs, growth, a sound government, and a sound economy—these are great and good goals. But they are not enough. Our prosperity means little if it lacks purpose. We diminish our triumph when we act as if wealth is an end in itself.

"The fact is that prosperity is not an end but a beginning. It has a point; it gives us time to think and care. It frees us up to learn, to grow, to be better than we are, to develop the things of the spirit and heart.

"Prosperity with a purpose means giving back to the country that has given you so much. It may mean helping a child from a dysfunctional home learn how to read, and teaching him through your presence that there is such a thing as health and reliable affection.

"It may mean taking your idealism and making it concrete by real action aimed at making life better for people. It may mean helping a church when it asks for volunteers. It may mean helping a civic group build a library or a local theater.

"Prosperity with a purpose may mean taking time after high school or college to serve and protect our nation in the armed forces of the United States.

"It means, in short, helping your brothers and sisters whoever they are, wherever they are, whatever their needs."

The Republican Party seems to be going through some sort of metamorphosis. Senator Dole is talking about the needs of people. Jack Kemp calls himself a "compassionate conservative." Republican theorists have always maintained that well-intentioned Democratic programs for the poor were counterproductive and that their own policies were ultimately the best for disadvantaged Americans. But now there's a difference. Party leaders are talking about people in need. They seem to have recognized that people are more interested in whether you care about them than they are in whether you are right.

"Our whole history as a party was protecting those who needed our help and making this a kinder nation.

"The party began by taking a stand for justice and personal decency—the end of slavery.

"It's a good trend.

"But I don't think that Republicans have a monopoly on caring, nor do Democrats. There are very sincere and concerned people in both parties. Unfortunately, there are selfish people too, and that's the reason we seem to have this ethical crisis.

"In recent years, success has become so important that some people have dropped their standards along the way. It's as if ethics were too heavy and would only slow their rise to the top. There's greed on Wall Street, graft in City Hall, and influence-peddling in Washington—and it's all shameful.

"Have we as a nation forgotten who we are? We're the people who sundered a nation rather than allow a sin called slavery. We're the people who together pushed past the snows and deserts of the West. And when we got there, what did we build, what did we care about? You could see the answer as you rode toward a new town and saw the silhouette against the sky. You would see just two buildings—a church and a schoolhouse. A place for the spirit and a place for our children to learn the great thoughts of man.

"We weren't saints, but we lived by standards.

"We celebrated the individual but we weren't self-centered. We were practical but we didn't live for material things. We believed in getting ahead but not through a narrow careerism.

"We were shrewd idealists, and we believed in big things. These days some of us act as if we've forgotten who we are. The truth is that we make ourselves small by pursuing small things. I find myself saying to my children, 'You've got to live by values if you want to live a life of meaning.'

"I have learned these past seven years that the Presidency provides an incomparable opportunity for moral leadership. A President must never intrude, but a President can set a tone, an atmosphere, a mood.

"I want to stand for new harmony, a greater tolerance. We have to remember that this country is and always has been a partnership.

"We need a new harmony, too, among the races in our country. The sadness of racial tensions in America should have ended by now. We are on a journey to a new century, and we must finally leave the tired old baggage of bigotry behind us.

"For all our faults, America is still a magnet for those people of the world who want a chance, who need a job, or who just don't want to be anywhere else in this 'American age.'

"To the many Hispanics who have joined us, let me say, 'You are not only welcome but needed. Who knows about family and faith better than you do? We need your leadership.' "

You have a reputation for maintaining hundreds of personal friends, people you correspond with and talk to on a regular basis. Your friends say you are thoughtful, always jotting little notes of recognition and encouragement. Is there a story behind this? Is there any methodology?

"No, there is no methodology, I believe in friendship. I've been blessed with many friends, and I think a relationship cuts two ways. You never take friends for granted.

"When my dad died, somebody wrote me a letter and said, 'When your dad dies you lose your best friend.' It made a tremendous impact on me. I was very close to my father and I loved him very much. That thoughtful little personal letter hit a chord right in my heart because it expressed how important both family and friendship are.

"I've been blessed through my life with close friendships, and they're my underpinning. When our son was sick, the thing that lifted us all up was faith and friendship. It transcends politics, crosses party lines, crosses ideologies.

"One of my closest friends in life is a former Democratic Congressman named Lud Ashley. I love him dearly. I remember that when our daughter was dying of cancer he was the guy sitting at her side. People would say to me, 'Hey, he votes against you on this or that.'

"I replied, 'I know, but he's my friend.' When we were hurting, there he was, lifting us up.

"You can't just go out and make friends; friendship is something that happens. I've been more blessed than most. People who really care are with you when you're up and are with you when you're getting kicked. Friends are really what makes life worthwhile."

- 3 -
A Matter of Faith

One of the major political news stories of 1985-86 was the evangelical Christian invasion of the Republican Party. In some counties and states, Republican leaders who had led the party for years were replaced by new evangelical activists. Riding just behind on a second wave was the Pat Robertson candidacy for the Republican nomination.

It was widely believed that the Vice President was caught off-guard by this phenomenon. But while it was true that many members of his staff underestimated just how great the evangelical wave would be, the Vice President himself had very wisely and accurately anticipated the potential problems and opportunities. As early as 1985 he was thinking of ways to keep the peace.

The evangelical challenge in the Republican Party was not unlike the situation that confronted Catholics and Democrats a hundred years earlier. In fact the parallels were striking.

For example, during a 50-year period, Catholic population in America increased from 17 percent to almost 40 percent as Irish, Polish, and Italian immigrants flooded North America. Similarly, between the 1950's and the 1980's the born-again evangelical population of Americans increased at almost the same rate.

The Catholic immigrants settled in northern Republican states, such as New York, Massachusetts, Rhode Island, and Pennsylvania, turning them into Democrat bastions, just as the new evangelicals concentrated in a Democratic South, turning it into Republican territory.

If today's evangelicals were conservative, so were the nineteenth-century immigrant Catholics. Motion pictures were censored, books were indexed, and on some occasions demonstrations were held on Broadway to shut down risqué theatrical performances. Like the new evangelicals, the Catholics were quite concerned with the education of their children. They had their own school systems, influenced the textbook industry, and organized politically to elect themselves onto local school boards. In the 1940's, Cardinal Spellman was so concerned with Bertrand Russell's agnosticism that he forced the professor's resignation from New York City College.

One of the lessons to be learned from the Catholic-Democrat experience was that one could expect great division and reaction. Anti-Catholic bigotry was inflamed and the Democratic Party was practically split asunder. As late as 1940, seven "Know-Nothings" were elected to the United States Congress, essentially running against the Catholic Church. It was an ugly time.

From a political standpoint, perhaps the most instructive lesson of all was that by humbling themselves the Democrats eventually welcomed the new Catholic political activists into their party and made them major players in one of the great political majorities in American history. The question was, Would the story be repeated? Would the Republican Party humble itself, put down its golf clubs, open its country club doors, and welcome the new evangelicals into the party?

The Vice President knew the challenges, but he also saw the opportunity. No one should ever be excluded from the process, and certainly not on the basis of his or her faith. The challenge was to both respect traditional Republicans who had worked hard and given their lives to build the party and at the same time welcome new recruits who were necessary to the process of forging a new majority.

In 1986, only hours before the Vice President left for Saudi Arabia, we conducted a videotaped interview at the BIZNET studios in downtown Washington D.C.

The idea was to get an account of the Vice President's faith on the record before the political season got hot and heavy. Just where did he stand on the issues? Before the studio lights were turned on, Marlin Fitzwater, the Vice President's popular new Press Secretary, pulled me aside and advised me to "shoot with both barrels." Abortion, prayer in school—nothing was off-limits. We all knew that the Vice President didn't talk much about his own personal faith, but Fitzwater encouraged me to plow right ahead. And so, even months before the new evangelical activists began flooding into the party in Michigan, Iowa, and South Carolina, the Vice President established for the record just where he stood on many of the issues that were soon to liven up the political debate.

So the interview began.

Last year the Democratic National Chairman sent thousands of letters across the country, suggesting that the evangelical movement represented a threat to the political process. The suggestion was that America's pluralism was in danger. How do you feel about the involvement of evangelicals in political life?

"I think the Democrats may have made a big mistake. The evangelical movement transcends party lines, and of course it should. I would hope that most evangelicals are Republicans, but I know from experience that many are Democrats, especially in the South.

"My view is that we should carefully respect the separation of church and state, but just as carefully defend the right of all people, including evangelicals, to participate in the process without intimidation or ridicule.

"I have made the point over and over again that the Democratic National Committee never complained when the clergy from the left got involved in protests over Vietnam and other causes. Even today they are silent when liberal churchmen fight us on aid to the freedom fighters. You never hear any complaints about church and state when they like the cause. But when evangelicals get fired up, for example, over an erosion in family values, then there is a great outcry from some on the Democratic National Committee. That's hypocritical.

"Separation of church and state? Yes. One nation under God? Yes—transcending even political party lines. But evangelicals, as all other Americans, have the right and even a responsibility to participate in the process, advocating their values. I support them. I think their involvement is healthy for America."

Let me ask you where you stand on some of the more controversial social issues.

"Fire away."

Prayer in schools?

"In 1969, as a member of Congress, I joined a number of others in introducing an amendment to the Constitution to provide voluntary prayer in schools. I believe in it and I think it's proper.

"Of course, I'm very sensitive to the fact that there are many people of a minority faith. They should not be intimidated or singled out or in any way put on the spot, but if it is voluntary, prayer in school could be accomplished with respect for all. I have supported it for a long time, the American people overwhelmingly want that right restored, and I would like to see progress in both houses of the Congress on this issue."

Abortion?

"As I mentioned in my debate with Geraldine Ferraro, this has been an evolving issue for me. And when I talk about it being an evolving issue, I am referring to the subject in a legal sense. Morally, I have long been opposed to abortion. The question has been, What is the best way to restore respect for the sanctity of life?

"Since the Supreme Court's Roe-versus-Wade decision in 1973 there have been about 18 million abortions in this country. That is a tragedy of shattering proportions. It brings a new sense of urgency to do something.

"I support a constitutional amendment that would reverse the Supreme Court's Roe-versus-Wade decision. I also support a human-life amendment with an exception for the life of the mother, rape, or incest. In addition, I oppose the use of federal funds to pay for abortion, except when the life of the mother is actually threatened."

Pornography?

"This administration has spoken out strongly against pornography. While we pride ourselves on the right of free speech and the right of the free press, my own view is that there are limits. When you have something that is clearly debilitating to society, undermining the moral values of this country, then we've got to find a way to deal with it. Commission after commission has come to this same conclusion.

Is there a spiritual side to George Bush?

"Yes, there is a spiritual side. I haven't always found it easy to discuss this in public, since my faith has been a very personal thing to me."

You were raised in a Christian home?

"My upbringing was very conventional Christianity. We had prayer at home and regular church attendance. There was never any doubt that Jesus Christ was my Savior and Lord. Even to this day, there has been a total conviction on this point.

"It's interesting that when you are in public life, people are always trying to put you into a conventional mold, to categorize you, but they seldom look beneath the surface to see what's in your heart. There have been so many personal moments."

You talked about being shot down over the Pacific.

"That certainly was one time. I was praying, crying out to God for help. And then there was this calm, this sense of faith, that somehow I was going to live. It was not a sudden thing, a seeing of the light, but rather an inner peace."

In 1984, in the Presidential debates, journalist Fred Barnes asked each candidate whether he or she had been born again. How would you answer the born-again question?

"I've discussed this many times with some of the great religious leaders, especially Billy Graham. I think I would ask for a definition. If by 'born again' one is asking, 'Do you accept Jesus Christ as your personal Savior?' then I could answer a clear-cut 'Yes.' No hesitancy, no awkwardness.

"But if one is asking, 'Has there been one single moment, above any others, in which your life has been instantly changed?' then I can't say that this has happened, since there have been *many* moments.

"I'm not a great biblical expert or theologian, but I am a *believer*. I do believe strongly in the Lord and the hereafter, in life after death."

Billy Graham is a friend of yours. Cardinal Law of Boston has stayed with you at the residence. Rabbi Tannenbaum is often photographed with you and mentioned as a friend. Jerry Falwell has endorsed you for the Presidency. So has Dr. Criswell of Dallas, Jack Stanton (Vice President of the Southern Baptist Convention), Ed McAteer (so-called founder of the religious right), and Bill Carmichael (evangelical publisher). What does all this mean? What influence do these religious leaders have on your life? What kind of influence should they have?

"I learn from all of them, even though we don't always agree on everything.

"For example, I have had some lively discussions with the former presiding Bishop of my own Episcopal church, Jack Allen. And yet Jack has always been a great source of strength to me.

"You mention Marc Tannenbaum. I remember Marc back in my U.N. days. Here was a courageous leader carrying the banner for the fate of Soviet Jewry.

"He's a man who has made a difference. He has helped a lot of people in this country see truth about the Soviet Union, and the truth about who we as Americans are as a people and a nation.

"This country was clearly born out of a desire for liberty and human rights, for the freedom to speak and assemble and worship, each in our own way. This is our heritage, one that we must never abandon for the expediency of the moment.

"We have stood for these values for 200 years. These are the very values embodied in the Helsinki Accords. And Marc Tannenbaum and others refuse to give up unless the Soviets fully comply with these values.

"It would be easier, safer, more diplomatic to remain silent, to negotiate our treaties and never raise the question of human rights. But that would be untrue to ourselves, and it would break our promise to the past.

"Let me tell you, I have been to Yad Vashem. And I have been to Auschwitz. I have seen the mounds of human hair, the eyeglasses, the toothbrushes, the tiny children's shoes— all that remains of the millions of victims who died there. I have seen the empty canisters of poison gas.

"These are the places that remind us that we cannot be silent. The lesson of these places is that never again can we remain silent about the abuse of human rights—never again.

"I came away from Auschwitz determined not just to remember the Holocaust but determined to renew our commitment to human rights around the world. I found myself thinking, 'If we in the United States are not strong enough, not courageous enough, to stand up for human rights, then who will? Who in God's name will?'

"As Elie Wiesel once said, 'In extreme situations, when human lives and dignity are at stake, neutrality is a sin.'

"I'll never forget the first time I met Avital Scharansky, the wife of the popular Soviet scientist Natan Scharansky. It was in Jerusalem eight years ago. She told me of receiving her exit visa one day after her wedding, of leaving her husband behind in Moscow, of the five years that had passed since they had parted. I can tell you, I was very moved.

"Yet seven more years would pass before Natan Scharansky would be freed, seven more years in which the President, Secretary Schultz, and I pressed his case at every opportunity. Seven more years before the Soviets finally opened up the gates and freed this champion of human dignity, his indomitable spirit still intact despite his years in the gulag.

"There are many others: Vladimir Slepak, Ida Nudel, Yuli Edelshtein, and countless more who have been left behind, many whose names we don't even know.

"Now Mr. Gorbachev has embarked on a policy of glasnost, or openness. But openness begins at the borders. I won't be content to see five or six or ten or 20 refuseniks released at a time, but thousands, tens of thousands—all those who want to go. And those who want to stay, let them practice their religion in freedom. Let them study Hebrew. Let them pray in their own synagogues. Let them hear the Voice of Israel broadcasts. Let them lead Jewish lives.

"The human-rights issue is now a permanent part of the U.S.-Soviet agenda. It was high on the agenda for the summit. I personally raised it with Mr. Gorbachev. And I can tell you, I will not be satisfied until the promise of Helsinki is a reality.

"Mr. Gorbachev: Let these people go!"

Jerry Falwell?

"When we went to Sudan, we visited Jerry Falwell's hospital. Here was the private sector, individual Christians, reaching out to deprived Muslims. I took Pat Robertson along on that trip, and it was very instructive, since his organization was also involved. Dan O'Neill and Mercy Corps International were there, as well as Ted Engstrom's World Vision organization. The evangelicals didn't wait for government to get involved; they saw people dying and they jumped in to help."

What influence do these people have?

"They are religious leaders who represent thousands of constituents. They have every right to offer input from their particular vantage point, though we don't agree on every issue. Why should we? Even Barbara and I don't agree on every issue. But certainly I want to be sensitive to their concerns."

You and Cardinal Law seem to see a lot of each other. How did that get started?

"I think we ended up on the same platform together in Atlanta, Georgia. If I remember correctly, it was a special memorial church service for Dr. Martin Luther King. We had quite an animated conversation, which I didn't want to end. As it turned out, we flew him back with us to Washington on Air Force Two and he ended up spending the night.

"Our relationship is not political and it shouldn't be. Barbara and I found this man to be more than a 'prince of the church'; he has a pastor's heart. It was a wonderful time. As you may know, Pio Laghi, the Vatican's Pro Nuncio, lives right across the street from us. The next morning the Cardinal and I walked over and said 'Hello.'

"One Fourth of July we had the Cardinal at Kennebunkport. It was hot—I'm sure they were sweltering in Boston! We had him out on the boat watching the firecrackers exploding in the summer sky.

"And then one time he took us on a little tour of some of his favorite places in his archdiocese. I think we visited a monastery.

"It's very moving to see people of faith going about their business, and at the same time to realize what a contribution they make to this country.

"I have to add this political note. I know that many Catholic political writers felt that they were being drummed out of the Democratic Party in 1972. Some of their most brilliant ideologues and some of their finest political intellectuals felt like they were getting the brush-off.

"I welcome their involvement in the Republican Party, just as I welcome the new-evangelical activists. We need to be inclusive, and certainly we need men and women of faith to give us their perspective.

"One of the great losses to American political life in this century was the withdrawal in the 20's of many religious leaders from active political involvement. When they left the political scene, they took with them their moral perspective and commitment, qualities that had helped shape our country from its earliest days.

"But even though many evangelicals left the political scene, the pastors of Black churches, to their great credit, took another route. They saw that political involvement could be of enormous importance to the bettering of the moral and spiritual life of their parishioners. They led the struggle for full civil rights for Black Americans. They continue to produce important leaders today.

"But in the last few years, in a great revival of an old American tradition, other fundamentalists have joined the Black pastors in taking an interest in politics.

"There is in our country, and must always remain, a wall between church and state. But there has never been and should never be a wall between church or synagogue and politics. Some people have lost sight of this truth, at least when they consider the political participation of conservative rather than liberal clergy. Fundamentalists, for example, have been accused of 'moral McCarthyism' and of engaging in dangerous political action, and have been the target of particular scorn in some quarters in the press.

"I believe it's all right for Reverend William Sloane Coffin to advocate very liberal political positions. I believe it was all right for the very liberal Father Robert Drinan to serve in Congress, although I wish we had defeated him.

"I don't get upset when I hear leaders of my own denomination speaking out through the National Council of Churches, even when they're 180 degrees off the mark. That's their right!

"But America also needs moral leaders who understand that the way to world peace is not through a weak America but a strong America, who understand that it is morally essential to maintain a strong American defense, who understand that our Strategic Defense Initiative is based on what is fundamentally a moral vision, a vision of a world free from the madness of nuclear terror, a vision of putting weapons at risk rather than people at risk. That's what we support, and that's the moral thing to do.

"America needs moral leaders who understand that Communism is evil and that those fighting against it for their freedom around the world have a fundamentally moral claim on our support. I'm talking about the freedom fighters in Afghanistan, Angola, Kampuchea, and Nicaragua. No people more deserve the aid of America than those heroic men and women.

"When I visited Guatemala for the inauguration of their new democratically-elected President, I ran into Commandante Daniel Ortega, the Nicaraguan dictator. He said that our own revolution had been violent, and therefore we should support him.

"I pointed out that the United States gave more support to the Sandinistas than any other country did right after they came to power while talking 'democracy.' They betrayed their own revolution. They turned their backs on free elections, on freedom of the press, and on individual freedoms. They harassed the Church and humiliated the Holy Father.

"I told Ortega that we were in Guatemala to honor democracy. Democracy is what we will support, and hopefully someday we will honor it in Nicaragua.

"A strong defense, the Strategic Defense Initiative, standing with freedom fighters around the world, continuing the battles for school prayer and against pornography, and also against abortion, continuing to create opportunity for all Americans, especially opportunity for young people to start a job or a business and to start a family—this is the continuing conservative agenda.

"America is in crying need of the moral vision that people of faith can bring to our political life—a vision of an America filled with hope and opportunity for all. A vision of an America that is confident of its fundamental message for all mankind. A message of hope. A message of love. A message of the rebirth of mankind in freedom and love of God.

"There's a line in an old song that with a slight change tells the vision and message that many people of faith share: 'As He died to make men holy, let us live to make men free.' We can't just walk away from our commitment as leaders of the free world."

A year later I ended up on a Vice Presidential swing through the South. On several occasions I was able to continue the same conversation.

Do you ever get into any theological discussions with some of the religious leaders?

"Sure. Not too many months ago I had several leaders over to the residence for a chat. There must have been five or six of them. Everett Stenhouse was there, as well as Charles Stanley, and Jerry Falwell.

"Dr. Stanley and I got into quite a discussion on just what constitutes salvation. You have to know Stanley. For a while he served as President of the Southern Baptist Convention, and that's what thrust him into the limelight. But really he is a pastor at heart.

"Soon we were involved pretty deeply in the old faith-versus-works debate, and I suppose I was arguing from the Episcopalian side of things. But the whole thing was over much too quickly for me. So we discuss theology when we're together. I guess I'm lucky to have a relationship with some of these great people."

Where does the Bush family worship?

"I'm a vestryman at St. Anne's in Kennebunkport, Maine. And we visit there on weekend trips to the Northeast. When we're home in Houston, we attend St. Martin's Episcopal Church.

"In Washington D.C. we move around quite a bit. Sometimes Barbara and I visit a Black Baptist church. Thad Garrett is the pastor there, and we really enjoy ourselves. Sometimes we stop by the National Cathedral."

You've been close to Jerry Falwell over the years.

"Barbara and I consider Jerry and Macell and their son Jonathan as our dear friends. I guess some people think that Jerry and I are sort of an odd couple. He has had friends criticize him for his strong support of me and I've had people telling me, 'Don't you know that Jerry Falwell hurts you politically?'

"In a way it's sad when a person becomes high-profile in this country. It's often hard to separate fact from fiction. Jerry Falwell has been an absolute gentleman to me. He's never asked for a thing, and he has only given encouragement and friendship."

Adrian Rogers?

"We have only just begun a dialogue. But I look forward to a long relationship. Here is a man whom the Southern Baptists have kept coming back to. He served them earlier as President of the Convention, and now again. On top of everything else, he pastors one of the largest churches in the world.

"The last time we were together he gave me some pretty frank and sobering advice on the necessity of involving evangelicals in the process. He feared that if the Republican Party shut their doors during the primaries, this great voter bloc would sit on its hands in the general elections. And of course I listened.

On the Evangelical Movement: "They not only have a right to participate, it's their responsibility. The nation needs their perspective."

When criticized for being "too loyal" to President Reagan, the Vice President says, "In my family, loyalty was never considered a character flaw."

"There are many who presume to speak for the evangelical movement, but surely Dr. Rogers is one of a handful who truly represent them. I would put Ben Armstrong of the Religious Broadcasters in that same category. And of course there are many others. Ed McAteer, the founder of the Religious Roundtable (and the man who some say was the founder of the whole Religious Right movement), is actually a member of Rogers' congregation. He is a great man with a lot of influence and a lot of wisdom. The Southern Baptists have more than 14 million members, and next to the Catholics are the largest denomination in America. And so they will have, and should have, some input into where the country is headed."

Robert Schuller?

"As I understand it, Dr. Schuller is like me in that he is not an easy man to categorize. He is a born-again Christian, but he has a very large following among Catholics, Jews, and people who aren't very religious at all, but just look to him for inspiration and encouragement in their lives.

"There's no doubt that Dr. Schuller has brought a lot of hope to a lot of people, as evidenced by the fact that year in and year out his books stay at the top of the *New York Times'* best-seller list. A couple of different times Barbara and I have tried to get out to the Crystal Cathedral, and I know it will happen someday. Meanwhile he and I exchange notes from time to time. Here is an example of a really bright man who refuses to be cynical."

Billy Graham is probably your oldest evangelical friend. When did that get started? What kind of impact has he had on your life?

"We really got to know each other during my years in Congress. And yes, our families are very close.

"Billy hasn't just impacted my own life; he has impacted all of us. We often spend time together in the summers up at Kennebunkport. Some nights I've stepped into a room and found my children seated around Billy asking questions about the Bible.

"So it's an old and close relationship, one that is very personal. Barbara and I are determined not to let it become politicized."

The Vice President's discretion in his relationship with Billy Graham soon became more intriguing to me than the relationship itself. I imagined that it was because there had been controversy in the Nixon-Graham relationship, and the Vice President wanted to respect Graham's right to put his ministry above politics. But the longer I observed the relationship, the more I became convinced that it was just as the Vice President had said. It was hard for men and women in public life to have friends as opposed to political allies. In some special way the Vice President and the evangelist were kindred spirits, and they didn't want to ruin that relationship.

World Vision President Ted Engstrom once told me, "Billy Graham says that George Bush is the best friend he has in the whole world outside his own immediate staff."

Besides their rendezvous at Kennebunkport, the two chat often by phone. One afternoon at the residence, the Vice President interrupted a conversation we were having together. "I think Billy Graham is in France today," he said, picking up the telephone. And soon the two of them were chatting. The evangelist was going on to Finland, and the Vice President insisted that Graham talk with the President of the government, who was his good friend.

Sometimes the Vice President would go to extraordinary lengths to protect the relationship. In 1986, with the political season heating up, he flew into the Carolinas, and during the trip the Bush-Graham relationship almost broke into the open.

"Some of the local party people down there arranged for me to go out to Billy Graham's house," the Vice President told me later. "They knew we were friends. It was a nice thing to do.

"But I called him up and said, 'Billy, there is nothing I would like better than to come out to your place, and see your home, and stand out on that famous patio, and touch all the things that you and Ruth love and hold dear. But I'm not going to do it.

" 'If I take that long motorcade out to your place with all those journalists, it will be all over the front pages tomorrow. I'm just not going to do it to you.' "

Of course the Vice President knew that an association with the evangelist would be very meaningful to evangelical Christians. Still, he was not about to use a friendship for his own political purposes.

George W. Bush, the Vice President's son:

"Billy Graham is one of the finest men I have ever met in my life. He comes up to Maine in the summertime.

"I remember one night when Dad asked Billy if he would sit around with the family and answer questions and just talk about his life and his view of things, his spirituality. It was one of the most exciting nights I have ever spent in my life. The man is powerful and yet humble. That combination of wisdom and humility was so inspiring to me individually that I took up the Bible in a more serious and meaningful way.

"As you know, one's walk in life is full of all kinds of little blind alleys. Sometimes life isn't easy, and so Billy redirected my way of thinking in a very positive way. He answered questions of all types.

"The next year when he came, he made it a point to call me aside and ask how things were going. He took a real interest in me individually, and for that I am forever grateful. It's an example of one man's impact on another person's life. And it was a very strong impact."

In July of 1986 the Vice President held a reception at the residence for a large group of religious leaders. Before things got started we were upstairs in a little working office next to his bedroom. A well-worn copy of C.S. Lewis' *Mere Christianity* was at the top of a stack of books on his desk. Lewis, the great Anglican Christian apologist and friend of J.R.R. Tolkien, was a favorite of evangelicals.

Do you read C.S. Lewis?

"Yes. People from different denominations are always recommending his books to me, and I always feel like saying, 'But he's Anglican. This is what we Episcopalians believe.'

"I'm learning that some Christians feel that it's very important to speak out about their faith. For them it is another religious tenet. They feel they are wrong if they don't stand up and say something.

"I have to balance that belief with my Episcopalian upbringing. C.S. Lewis taught that the greatest sin is pride, and that all other sins really come from pride. So we haven't been inclined to go around proclaiming that we are Christians. It somehow smacked of self-righteousness to us. Why do we have to tell people something that our own lives should demonstrate? It seemed prideful. But I must say that Barbara and I have talked about it, and we are learning that there are two sides to this."

Have you ever been disillusioned with your faith?

"We really went through a tough time with the loss of Robin. Imagine being told one day by the doctors that your little three-year-old girl has leukemia and will die within weeks.

"I can tell you that there was no one for us to turn to but God. And I really learned to pray. I would slip into our church sometimes when no one was there. I would ask God, 'Why? Why this little innocent girl?'

"We lost Robin, but Barbara and I have never lost the faith and spiritual insight from that experience. I don't really think it was disillusioning. Actually, the pain of that experience taught us just how dependent on God we really are, and how important our faith is. In a moment like that, all you have is God."

- 4 -
Facing Up to the Soviets

In the summer and fall of 1987, public opinion polls once again showed the Vice President leading the pack as the nation's first choice to be the next President. Characteristically, Washington political pros concluded that it was not to be. If recent history had taught anything about Presidential politics, it had taught that the expected never happened. Consequently there weren't many newspaper columns analyzing a possible Bush Presidency.

I was curious: What kind of President would he make? In what direction would he take the country?

To appreciate where a George Bush Presidency would go, one must consider where the trail began and how it would lead to the door of the White House.

Historically, most nominees for the highest office in the land had been the products of a political machine. Sometimes this had worked quite well, as for Abraham Lincoln or Harry Truman. But since Watergate the American people have been rejecting "machine" candidates, with a recent example being Walter Mondale.

Indeed, "antiestablishmentarianism" had become quite the vogue in this generation of Presidential politics. Political figures of such diverse ideology as Eugene McCarthy and George Wallace had built national constituencies by "running against Washington." Jimmy Carter was the "outsider," even in his own party, and in some respects the early Democratic front-runner for 1988, Gary Hart, had been maintaining a similar tone by keeping some distance between himself and labor, and other traditional powers of the Democratic Party. Another long-shot possibility, Lee Iaccoca, had been popular precisely because he came from the private sector and could presumably "go back there and fix things up like a businessman."

Other recent nominees had been the leaders of various political/philosophical movements. George McGovern, for example, started from a virtually nonexistent political base in South Dakota and became the spokesman of the liberal antiwar movement, riding the crest to his party's nomination in 1972. Ronald Reagan had led the conservative movement to power in 1980.

All of this brought me to George Bush. He was not the product of a political machine, as a Kennedy or Humphrey or Nixon. He was certainly not an antiestablishment figure, as Jimmy Carter. And he was not the leader of a passionate political/philosophical movement, as Reagan or McGovern. Then how had he become the credible front-runner? Into which category would he fit?

The answer was that George Bush could be called a "diplomat President." Though his extraordinary governmental experience had ranged across many departments, his star had risen mainly through a successful diplomatic career. It was his role as the U.N. Ambassador, as special representative to the People's Republic of China, and as the Director of the CIA that had thrust him into the national and international limelight.

This was a unique political phenomenon the likes of which we hadn't seen since such early household American names as John Adams, Thomas Jefferson, James Madison, and James Monroe. Indeed, most of our early Presidents had been diplomats, gaining preparation for the job as Ambassadors to Great Britain or France. Several had served as Secretaries of State. Most of the early Presidents had never served in the Senate or as Governors.

These first "diplomat Presidents" had been born out of necessity. The new country was still so small and weak that its very existence depended on economic and military cooperation with European powers. Within time, a combination of growing American self-sufficiency and easily maintained borders (which included the vast defenses of the Atlantic and Pacific oceans) had given us the security we needed. America turned inward.

One could make the case that during the ensuing two centuries our situation had completed the full cycle. Third World powers were now forming economic cartels. Europe and Japan were proving to be formidable free-market competitors, and Soviet missiles were able to cross the mighty oceans in 15 minutes. One could make a good argument that necessity once more demanded a "diplomat President"—that if George Bush didn't exist, we would have to make him up, and that Presidents of the future would need foreign policy experience. Our most urgent problems, ranging from the budget and trade deficits to stopping the international drug trade, depended on such expertise.

A couple of times during the fall of 1987 I stopped by the Vice President's residence and talked to him about where America was drifting in international waters, and just what our priorities should be.

"Politics and foreign policy aren't so different from combat. Sure, there's a place for brilliant concepts and strategies and tactics. But bright ideas can fail if they aren't carried out by people who know who they are and what they want, people who know how to persevere and how to stand up under pressure. Steadiness, courage, and character—those are the real keys to success in any serious endeavor.

"I'm proud of the fact that for the past seven years our administration has taken a steady and resolute approach in our relationship with the Soviet Union. As a result of that strength we are on the verge of a truly historic agreement that mutually and verifiably reduces nuclear weapons—not merely *limits* but actually *reduces* those weapons.

"In the world today there is one simple and overriding moral imperative: We've got to keep from blowing each other up.

"In the years ahead there are many ways that we can build on the progress we've made. If we can agree to reduce nuclear weapons, then we can find a way to verifiably eliminate chemical and biological weapons. Such terrible weapons have no place in a civilized world. They should be banned from the face of the earth.

"This means that we have to keep talking and trying to negotiate with our adversaries. But it doesn't mean that we should let them manipulate public opinion with propaganda and political ploys or cut a deal that helps them and hurts us. We have to be tough as nails when we bargain with them, and we can't leave anything to trust.

"There is a long, proven record of what works with the Soviets. I firmly believe in talking with our adversaries, of airing our differences across a table. But a President must never negotiate from a position of weakness, and I never will. Peace and strength go hand-in-hand.

"What would the Democrats do? Cut back defense unilaterally and leave us nothing to bargain with. You can be sure of this: I will deal from strength or I won't deal at all."

Some conservatives are concerned about the verifiability of any treaty with the Soviet Union.

"That's a valid point; there must be verifiability. In the Ford Administration I was Director of the CIA, and I wear that as a badge of honor. That job opened my eyes to the world as it is, not as we might want it to be. The world is complicated and extremely dangerous. We need an intelligence capability that is second to none, and we need the ability to take covert actions to protect our national interests.

George Bush and Soviet leader Mikhail Gorbachev in Moscow.

George Bush with Chancellor Helmut Kohl of West Germany. During the last seven years as Vice President, George Bush visited the 50 States, 74 foreign countries, and five U.S. possessions, flying over one million miles.

"No matter what the liberals in Congress think, we must protect our sources and methods of intelligence. We must find a way to curtail damaging leaks. The CIA is absolutely essential to our national security, and we need to strengthen it, not weaken it.

"As the nation's chief intelligence officer, I saw the reality of Soviet intentions, and how they are cloaked by disinformation and propaganda.

"For example, in arms negotiations, the Soviets' overt agenda is to reduce nuclear weapons. We share that goal. But the Soviets' *covert* agenda, their unstated objective, is twofold: They want to drive a wedge between us and our allies, and they want to weaken the defenses of Western Europe.

"Our position on these points is loud and clear: NATO is the cornerstone of our national security policy, of our strategy for peace. We will not allow the Soviets to split the alliance or to weaken it."

In 1981 stories were making the rounds in Washington that you had practically held NATO together, that your trip at that time was pivotal. How will the NATO nations come through this INF process?

"NATO is stronger than ever, and there is an important lesson in this. Four years ago, in an earlier phase of the arms talks now going on in Geneva, I had the job of consulting with our NATO partners on the issues involved. I met with our allied leaders and explained that we had to counter the Soviet monopoly in intermediate-range nuclear weapons, either by deploying Pershing II missiles and cruise missiles in Western Europe or else by banning an entire category of weapons.

"When the Soviets did not respond to the latter proposal, the Zero Option, West Germany deployed our Pershing II missiles in the face of emotional and even violent domestic protests.

"When I returned to West Germany in July of that year, demonstrators charged and stoned our motorcade. They literally attacked the car that Chancellor Kohl and I and our wives were riding in. It was an ugly incident. And it brought home to me just what our friends in NATO were up against and how steadfast they had been.

"But because of that steadiness, Europe and the United States scored a great victory. Four years ago the Soviet Union was trying to convince NATO to disarm unilaterally. Today, with the Soviet Union facing a unified Western Europe and America, we are negotiating mutual and verifiable arms reductions.

"All of this carries an important lesson. Strength and solidarity are the linchpins of our NATO alliance. They are what brought the Soviets to the bargaining table to negotiate seriously. And they are just what we will need after an arms agreement to counter the Warsaw Pact edge in conventional forces."

Of course, now all the presidential candidates are calling for cutbacks in defense.

"There are savings we can make—in procurements, for example—but President Reagan has pointed out time and again that if our country is not safe, discussing the other hotly debated issues of the day is irrelevant. We have long understood that if freedom is to survive anywhere, it depends on the strength, security, and determination of our country.

"Thomas Jefferson once said, 'We must do our duty and convince the world that we are just friends and brave enemies.' It's hard to do this because some people in Washington seem confused as to which countries are the friends and which countries are the enemies of the United States.

"In a world filled with tyrants and lunatics, in a world of Castros and Qaddafis, in a world where Afghan villages are being destroyed with chilling efficiency, we cannot afford to be governed by people possessed by the overwhelming obsession to apologize for the United States.

"The voters of the United States have rejected what Jeanne Kirkpatrick rightly calls the 'blame-America-first' crowd. And the American people don't buy the idea that the United States is morally equivalent to any country which denies its citizens the right to speak or assemble and declares the worship of God to be a social evil."

When one thinks of strategic weapons, one thinks of decades for development. Yet we seem to have turned things around pretty quickly. Obviously the Soviets are willing to slow down the arms race now, since they sense an American comeback.

"When the President and I came to Washington at the end of the decade, our strategic systems were being treated like government employees during a budget squeeze. New systems were not being brought on line, and those retired were not being replaced. The B-1 bomber, for example, was canceled unilaterally. No serious attempt had been made to secure a 'quid pro quo' from the Soviets. That left the Soviets with powerful new Backfire bombers and our own aircrews in B-52's, planes which were often older than the pilots.

"We went to work repairing the damage and putting America back on the path to security. We started the production line on the B-1. We saved the MX missile. We stood firm with our European allies, proceeding with the installation of Cruise and Pershing II missiles, thereby countering the deployment of Soviet SS-20's. And we proved European public opinion wrong. They had said that the NATO deployment would guarantee no arms talks with the Soviets. But our firmness brought them to the table.

"President Reagan has set in motion a program that I predict will be heralded in the years ahead as one of the twentieth century's giant steps forward. We have mobilized our scientists to develop the technology for a system designed to protect people rather than kill them.

"Just as the Zero Option for eliminating intermediate-range nuclear forces had strong moral underpinnings, SDI likewise has strong moral underpinnings: Put *weapons* at risk rather than people. As technology has moved, we should move to a concept that emphasizes defense and not just mutual destruction.

"President Reagan's vision and his political courage to stand his ground have created a historic turning point."

Yet some people are saying that we face serious danger with inadequate conventional forces.

"It's true that strategic forces were not the only part of America's arsenal that was neglected in the 1970's. When we got to Washington, we made a major commitment to rebuild the conventional strength of our military. Here too much has been accomplished. We are well on our way to our goal of a 600-ship Navy. Our other armed forces have also been beefed up, with everything from new tanks to additional spare parts.

"We continue to face major challenges in winning a national consensus behind our effort to rebuild America's defenses. But the President and I are determined that the taxpayer get full value for every defense dollar. The brave men and women who fill the ranks of our armed services deserve nothing less than the best in equipment and organizational leadership. The President picked a group of acknowledged experts under David Packard to give us recommendations on the critical issues. If there are ways to do the job better, ways to do the job for less money, we want to know what they are and then put them in place.

"Of course, the human factor is still the most important element in our nation's security. Let me tell you about the people who are making it their job to keep our country safe and at peace. I've visited them all over the world, and there is no doubt that we've got the best young people in the military today that we've ever had. They are top-quality, well-educated individuals dedicated to the protection of our country and our way of life. And today they have no doubt that their President and their fellow citizens back them up.

"I had the pleasure of meeting the crew of the *USS Yorktown*, a state-of-the-art battle cruiser. Eager and intelligent, these people exemplify the best that our Navy and our country has to offer. I thank God that the American people enthusiastically support those who wear the uniform in pride."

There has been some concern that we are overspending on defense technology. Even some conservatives have been critical of this, feeling that we can cut back without hurting our defense. Today's enemy is seen as the terrorist more than the conventional armed forces.

"We are dealing with these threats realistically. Unfortunately, here again we have been playing catch-up for past mistakes.

"First on the list in countering terrorism is an efficient, well-equipped intelligence system, manned by professionals and backed up by the political establishment. When terrorists' bombs go off, don't forget that ten years ago some people right here at home declared open season on the CIA. Patriotic individuals who had risked their lives for our country were treated like criminals. Ill-informed investigators with no regard for the protection of classified material joined renegades in a search-and-destroy mission against our most sensitive and vital intelligence capabilities. They leaked information and lists of names, and some of them even ripped the cover off loyal Americans who were risking their lives for their country. The result? Richard Welch gunned down in Athens and many of our most vital sources of intelligence lost.

"This travesty, like the denigration of our military which happened during the same period, is a dark chapter in our history. As a former director of the CIA, I can tell you that some of the difficulties we are now having to overcome in bringing terrorism under control can be traced to the excesses of those who devastated our intelligence system with their illegal disclosures a decade ago.

"The administration has moved decisively to rebuild America's intelligence community, especially bringing in top-quality people to make up for those who left in dismay during those dark years. Domestically, under Attorney General Meese's direction, we're on the offensive against espionage.

"On the international scale, our task is growing increasingly important. The Western democracies are engaged in an epic struggle with international terrorists. Free people cannot and will not stand by and watch a man in a wheelchair shot and thrown into the sea or American children gunned down at airports. Natasha Simpson, Leon Klinghoffer, and Robert Dean Stethem will not be forgotten.

"Teddy Roosevelt once said, 'The American people are slow to wrath, but once kindled it burns like a consuming flame.' "

Some problems defy resolution. One could agree that there will always be terrorism. The Irish conflict is almost eight centuries old, and certainly the Middle Eastern problems are older than that. How can anyone have hope? Is there any real prospect of resolving the Palestinian problem, for example?

Vice President Bush with Western European forces in February 1983. "Strength and solidarity are the linchpins of our NATO alliance."

Appointed Chief of the U.S. Liaison Office in Beijing, People's Republic of China, in 1974, George Bush returns 12 years later as Vice President. Shown here with Chinese leader Deng Xiaoping.

Dave Valdez, The White House

"We may never solve all the problems in the Middle East, and even if we now win the peace, problems may resurface in future generations. Yet there is a chance for peace for this generation in the Middle East. The underpinning for this hope is President Reagan's plan of September 1983, in which we addressed ourselves to the Palestinians' West Bank situation. We were talking in our plan of a confederation with Jordan. In my view we will not have lasting peace in the Middle East until the West Bank problem has been solved.

"We must continue to find a way to be a catalyst for peace. Israel is our strong friend and ally, and they have our wholehearted support. They have our commitment in that we will always see that they have a qualitative edge over any combination of states that might threaten them in the area. But they also know that we are committed to direct negotiations between Israel and their neighbors.

"Our policy of support for the moderate Arab states is designed to create more Sadats and fewer Qaddafis, more Husseins and fewer radicals like those running Iran. And so I say that there is hope for peace. We can't rest until peace is achieved, but it will not be achieved by U.S. dictation. It will only be achieved by direct negotiation between the parties in the area."

You're headed for Europe again soon. What will the message be this time?

"I'll be discussing the future of our alliance with the leaders of West Germany, France, and Great Britain. They are both our friends and our economic competitors. In planning the common defense of Europe, we must ensure that they carry their fair share of the load. And we must let them know that no new isolation will ever cause us to pull back from NATO.

"I will be going to Poland to talk with their leaders as well, and to meet with the courageous members of Solidarity who have caused the winds of change to blow in that land."

You mentioned SDI. How does "Star Wars" fit into all this? Are we going to keep pursuing the research in spite of the expense?

"The Soviets have been working on strategic defenses, including SDI-type technologies, much longer and harder than we have—in fact well before my time at the CIA in the mid-70's.

"They don't like the fact that the United States has an SDI research program of its own. They want to keep a monopoly on strategic defense, and they have made a major effort to accomplish that goal at the negotiating table. But they will not succeed. Like President Reagan, I strongly support this research because it will give us a defensive shield that puts *weapons* at risk rather than people.

"By relying on retaliation as a deterrent to attack, we limit our ability to deal with certain dangers—for example, an errant missile or a misinterpreted threat. It is both moral and logical to look for a better solution than mutually assured destruction. I prefer a policy of mutually assured survival."

What does the Gorbachev era represent for us?

"We will face challenge and change in our dealings with the Soviets. Mr. Gorbachev represents a generational change in the Soviet Union and the beginning of a new era in our relations.

"I was the first senior U.S. official to meet Chairman Gorbachev after he came to power in 1985. So I had that early opportunity to talk with him and take his measure.

"He is a new kind of Soviet leader—more open, more Western, and more knowledgeable about the world than his predecessors. That's good, I think, because it allows us to have a broader, more meaningful dialogue.

"He is an impressive man—self-confident, articulate, and obviously intelligent. But he is no pussycat. He is an orthodox, committed Marxist, and he will be a formidable and determined competitor for world power.

"Andrei Gromyko, the Soviet Foreign Minister for many years, accurately characterized Mr. Gorbachev at the time he took power: 'Comrades, this man has a nice smile, but he's got iron teeth.'

"Recently Mr. Gorbachev has embarked on a program of 'glasnost' or openness in an effort to lubricate Soviet joints that have been rusted shut as long as the Tin Man's in the Wizard of Oz.

"I am glad to see the change. I hope these internal reforms lead to a better life for the Soviet people. I hope they lead to more freedom, more opportunity, less oppression, less fear, and less intervention in the affairs of other countries such as Afghanistan and Nicaragua.

"If Gorbachev can succeed in transforming Soviet society, we will be waiting for him at the door of a new century, ready to move from an era of confrontation to one of cooperation. In a peaceful competition between our economies and ideologies, I am confident we will prevail.

"But let's not be naive. Let's not be carried away with the euphoric hope of instant democracy. The Soviets have very far to go.

"For the sake of the Soviet people, for whom we have no animosity at all, I hope this glasnost is just a beginning. Let's hope and pray that is the case, but let's keep our eyes wide open. *Caution* is our watchword, 'steady as she goes.'"

What are the dangers?

"We need to make sure that our yearning for peace does not become an acquiescence to injustice. We have to pursue peace wisely and deliberately and resist the clamor for a deal. We have to know how to avoid confusing status quo for stability.

"There are those who say that all is well, that everything has changed in the Soviet Union. Maybe they're right and maybe they're wrong—history will tell. But as we wait for history to render judgment, a prudent skepticism is in order.

"We must recommit ourselves to a doctrine that expresses the best in our history and our heritage. We must be true to the knowledge that the interests of the world are best served and the cause of peace is best served, not merely by containing Communism but by spreading freedom."

- 5 -
Taking On the Terrorists

When your administration came to power we were finding ourselves being drawn into a civil war in El Salvador. Neighboring Nicaragua with the help of Soviet and Cuban advisors in arms was exporting revolution. Today the story is all Nicaragua. El Salvador is much more secure because the Nicaraguans are preoccupied with securing their own regime. We have funded the Contras or freedom fighters in that country, and the Sandinistas have less resources and time to cause trouble in the region.

Is this a calculated policy? Is this some new Pentagon-State Department economics? Everyone knows that it is cheaper to destabilize a bad regime than it is to defend a good one. It seems that for the past generation we have been pouring billions of dollars into defending the free world. Now the tide seems to have turned. The Soviets are trying to defend regimes in Africa, Central America, and Asia. There is a war in Cambodia and in Afghanistan. Everywhere revolutionaries are battling the frontiers of what Jack Kemp calls the "Soviet Colonial Empire."

"I think the calculated policy can best be summed up by one word: *Democracy.*

"Let me be very specific: I intend to help the freedom fighters of the world to win their liberty. In the hills of Afghanistan and in the plains of Africa, we are on their side. And in Nicaragua we will help the Contras win democracy. This doctrine of democracy must be championed.

"Not too long ago the President invited five little children from Afghanistan to the Oval Office. It was enough to bring tears to your eyes. They could have been neighborhood children playing in the backyard with your kids. Only these young ones had been maimed and crippled because someone had bombed their neighborhoods and dropped booby traps designed specifically to entice children. These innocent children are the victims of the new Soviet imperialism.

"In Afghanistan, in Nicaragua, and in Angola, brave and courageous people are fighting the same enemy. I think one of our administration's greatest achievements has been opening the eyes of the American people, and the people of the Western democracies, to the moral power we share as free people. Whittaker Chambers once wrote, 'The success of Communism is never greater than the failure of all other faiths.'

"President Reagan has reignited in our people that faith in human freedom which is the heart of our society. Free people everywhere are part of the same family, and as part of the same family we must stand together. This is a power against which no tyrant, no terrorist, no despot of right or left can hope to prevail.

"Dr. Savimbi of Angola once said something really significant. Two years ago Jack Wheeler, an American pro-freedom activist, trekked into Angola to meet with him. In the interview which was later published in the United States, Dr. Savimbi told him, 'It is the Third World that has to give the West the courage to oppose the Soviet Union and to stand up for its ideas, not the other way around.'

"Now that's courage. We've got to support the people of Angola who are fighting for liberty and independence. They stood firm when the odds were overwhelmingly against them. Their strength of character inspired us. Let no one doubt, as President Reagan has put it, that their cause is our cause."

*Let's talk about Central America. What's at stake? Some
people think we may be overreacting to the problem.*

"I don't think we're overreacting at all. In Central America our stand for democracy is being severely tested. In one country, El Salvador, we did the right thing, and the result was freedom.

"In 1982 El Salvador was at a crossroads. To combat pressure from Soviet-supplied and Cuba-supplied infiltrators coming in from Nicaragua, the Salvadoran military was resorting to repressive tactics against their own people.

"At President Reagan's request I went there and met with the top Salvadoran military commanders. I told them that the United States would give them military and economic aid to meet the Nicaraguan threat, but I also told them bluntly that our cause was democracy, human rights, and individual freedom for the people of El Salvador. I told them they had to respect the law, guarantee fair trials, and hold free elections, and that if they didn't do those things they would lose U.S. support.

"Well, the El Salvadoran government was tough—tough enough to restore the rule of law. Abuses were curtailed and El Salvador, with our help, made the transition to a strong, vibrant, democratically-elected civilian government. And other countries have had similar experiences. Just last year I represented the United States at the inauguration of the democratically-elected Presidents in Guatemala and Honduras. These countries face enormous problems, but they're going down democracy road.

"These tremendous strides would never have been made had the United States ignored the military threat to that region. Military aid to El Salvador passed by only a few votes, yet it made all the difference."

And in Nicaragua?

"We support the Contras, the freedom fighters. Their struggle goes on in the hills outside Managua, and on the hill in Washington on which rests our U.S. Capitol.

"And here's what the struggle is about: It's about a small clique of political terrorists called the Sandinistas, who hijacked the Nicaraguan revolution, betrayed the patriots who fought and died for freedom, and put a Communist regime in the place where a democratic government was supposed to be. What they did is really tragic. They made Nicaragua a totalitarian state again, except that this time it was a dictatorship.

"Since taking control in 1979, the Sandinistas have done everything in their power to convert that country into a Marxist satellite. They have suspended civil liberties, muzzled the press, subverted free elections, hounded fundamentalist Christians, and trampled on the Catholic Church. They have closed down the Church radio and the Church newspaper. They have taunted and insulted the Pope.

"You don't have to think very hard to figure out why all this attention is paid to the Christian churches. Lech Walesa and his people in the Polish Solidarity movement march behind a crucifix, and Cory Aquino and her people stopped tanks by standing in the streets and praying. The day her people liberated the government television station, they placed prominently on the set a statue of the Mother of our Lord."

Some say the Sandinistas should be given a chance, that they represent a better choice, that their "liberation theology" is more compassionate than pure Marxism and a better alternative than the right-wing dictatorships that are so prevalent in Latin America.

"It's pretty astonishing to see these people who can't come to grips with who the Sandinistas are. The Sandinistas don't even bother to hide it. Ortega comes up to

New York City and buys designer eyeglasses so he won't look like what he is, but he still talks what he is. 'Marxist Leninism is the guide of Sandinismo,' Ortega says. Now that's pretty candid!

"There are Nicaraguan postage stamps of Lenin. There's a whole series of Marx, with the Communist Manifesto. They call him Carlos Marx—nice local touch! These aren't the only stamps they issue, but they're the ones that betray the true nature of the Sandinistas.

"I showed them to a European socialist Prime Minister of a country friendly to us. He pondered for a minute and said, 'Well, Marx had some good ideas.' I replied, 'Really? Well, democracy wasn't one of them.'

"If we allow the Sandinistas to proceed unopposed we can predict with absolute certainty what will happen: They will go about happily spreading their revolution and destabilizing their peaceful neighbors. They will bring perpetual war to Central America and untold hardship and pain to its people. And they will create what Communism always creates—a huge refugee machine.

"Is there no answer? There *is* an answer, and it's the freedom fighters who are out there in the hills fighting every day to give peace and democracy a chance. But just as some people refuse to admit who the Sandinistas are, others refuse to admit who the freedom fighters are.

"These courageous freedom fighters have been struggling to free their native Nicaragua. They have been putting their lives on the line against a massively armed foe because they believe in man's right to worship God, to speak, to own property, to direct the course of government through democratic elections.

"Some time ago George McGovern wrote a column for a major newspaper characterizing the armed resistance against the Sandinista dictatorship as being largely made up of 'the corrupt and brutal national guardsmen of the late and unlamented Anastasio Somoza.' What planet is this man living on?

"Many of those fighting the Sandinistas fought against Somoza. The majority of those bearing arms against the Sandinistas were in their early teens or younger during Somoza's reign. It is the betrayals and brutality of the Sandinistas that drive these brave individuals, often inadequately armed, into combat against one of the best-equipped armies in the hemisphere.

"Since 1980 the Sandinista regular army has gone from 10,000 to 70,000 strong. The Soviet Union has provided them 150 main battle tanks, 200 other armored vehicles, 45 fixed-wing aircraft, and 25 helicopters, including the latest deadly gunships. Who could question the cause of the brave individuals who are standing up to this kind of military machine?

"We want to help in the right way and at the right time—and that's now. We don't want to ever send U.S. troops there. There's no reason for our soldiers to fight there. They've got their own men and women in the field. The freedom fighters don't want us to fight for them, and they don't even want us to fight beside them.

"They're asking us for financial help—money for medical supplies, clothing, food, and yes, for guns and bullets. We've asked for a hundred million dollars, and if you want to be selfish about it I'll point out that a hundred million is nothing compared to what it will cost us if a few years from now we have to deal with millions of refugees."

Why the big fuss over a hundred million dollars to the Contras? The Soviets must spend more than that every month for the Sandinistas. Does a hundred million dollars really make a big difference? Isn't it a relatively small amount of money for the administration to fight about?

"There shouldn't be a storm over it because we should give it charitably and freely to those who are willing to fight Democracy's battle.

"I can't tell you that a hundred million dollars is going to solve the problem, but I can tell you that without support from the United States the freedom fighters will collapse and the Soviet-backed Sandinistas, the Marxist-Leninists, will solidify their totalitarian system. And they will continue to export their revolution into El Salvador, continue to threaten Costa Rica, and continue to threaten Honduras."

Will it work? Can we finance freedom fighters and expect them to really prevail?

"We're asking Congress for just enough help to give the Contras a chance. We've done it before, and it worked. In the early days of World War II, FDR wrote Churchill and tried to lift his spirits and the spirits of his countrymen. Churchill read FDR's kind words and later answered them: 'Give us the tools and we'll finish the job.'

"It's time to give the freedom fighters of Nicaragua the tools to rebuild democracy. I hope we Americans haven't forgotten that democracy doesn't belong just to us, the favored few.

"They deserved freedom in the Philippines, and when Marcos so corrupted the election process that the Filipino people threw him out, we were the first government to recognize the new government and pledge our support to it.

"They deserve freedom in Haiti, and when the Haitians brought down the dictator Duvalier we told them that we would do everything we could to help them get democracy rolling. The work is started there, but it isn't done yet.

"They deserve freedom in Nicaragua, and we're going to help them get it."

There's been a lot of controversy about the Iran arms-and-hostages deal. You were the first person in the administration to come forward and call it a mistake. And yet you've been criticized for not revealing your own counsel to the President during the event. What was the rationale? Where was the administration wanting to go with the initiative?

"The President was trying to open channels with a regime that all Americans despise. It was a risky business. When it became publicly known, there were immediate questions of how we could have a policy of not sending arms to Iran and then seemingly doing just the opposite. And of course there were questions about the operation of the National Security Council staff.

"Let me start with one basic concern. Why did we open a dialogue with Iran?

"Here was a country that deeply humiliated the United States by kidnapping our diplomats and burning our flag. We all remember blindfolded Americans being paraded around our own embassy in Tehran. There is in the hearts of the American people an understandable animosity to Khomeini's Iran. I feel that way myself, to be very honest with you, and so does the President, who has been vilified time and time again by Iran's radical leaders. We're told that most Iranians feel the same way about us, the country that they call the Great Satan.

"So why have anything to do with them? If you look at a map, Iran is all that stands between Soviets and the Gulf oil states. It's all that stands between the Soviets and a warmwater port. Either a disintegrating Iran or an overly powerful Iran could threaten the stability of the entire Middle East, and especially the moderate Arab states, our friends whose stability and independence are absolutely vital to the national security of the United States. We may not like the current Iranian regime, and I've said we don't, but it would be irresponsible to ignore its geopolitical and strategic importance.

"But of course this doesn't mean we should simply appease any Iranian regime. It does mean, however, that we

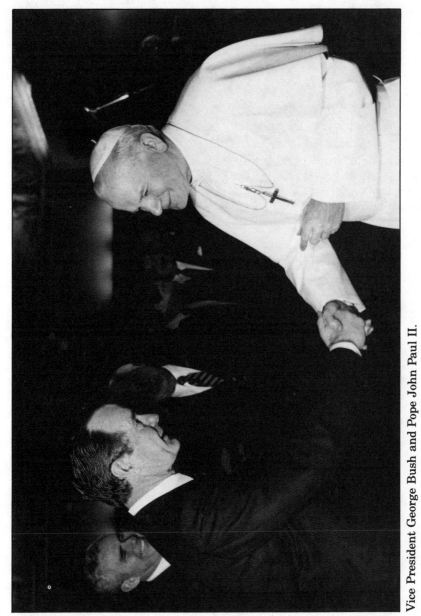

Dave Valdez, The White House

Vice President George Bush and Pope John Paul II.

George and Barbara Bush with Denis and Margaret Thatcher. The Vice President considers Margaret Thatcher to be one of Great Britain's greatest Prime Ministers and a "personal friend."

can't ignore this looming transition that will soon take place in Iran. Khomeini will pass from the scene. A successor regime will take power, and we must be positioned to serve America's interests, and indeed the interests of the entire free world.

"Apart from the strategic reasons, humanitarian concern about American hostages in Lebanon provided another reason to open a channel to Iran. The Iranians themselves were not holding our hostages, but we believed that they had influence over those who did.

"Let me add something very important: In spite of our bitter feelings toward Iran's leadership, we would have tried to begin a dialogue with Iran whether we had hostages in Lebanon or not. In fact, for three years prior to the first hostage kidnappings, this administration attempted to find reliable, hopefully moderate, Iranian channels through which to conduct a responsible dialogue."

Why moderates in a Khomeini regime? One can understand that there would be theological moderates, but wasn't the administration misled into thinking there were some Islamic leaders in positions of power who were sympathetic to the United States?

"For some time we were receiving intelligence that pragmatic elements within Iran were beginning to appreciate certain sobering realities. To the east in Afghanistan, we estimate that 115,000 Soviet troops are committing atrocities on Iran's Islamic brothers. To the north are 26 Soviet divisions, right there on Iran's border, for whatever opportunities might arise.

"To the west, Iran is engaged in a war with Iraq of unbelievably horrible human dimensions. Twelve-year-old kids are being pressed into service and then ground up in combat. At home, Iran is teetering on the economic brink right there in its own front yard, with a 40 percent unemployment rate. Many Iranian leaders understand that their own survival, and certainly the rebuilding of their economy, may depend on normalizing ties with their neighbors and with the Western world.

"So we for our own reasons, and certain elements in Iran for their own reasons (in spite of this mutual hatred), began a tentative, probing dialogue."

How did the arms shipments get involved?

"When we started talking to the Iranians, both sides were deeply suspicious of each other. Those Iranians who were taking enormous personal risks by just talking to us felt that they needed a signal from us that their risks were worth it. We were told the signal they required, and we gave them that signal by selling a limited amount of arms, about one-tenth of one percent of the arms that have been supplied by other countries.

"Likewise, we needed proof of Iranian seriousness. We required signs of a cessation of Iranian use of terrorism and help in gaining the release of our hostages in Lebanon. And we did see certain positive signs. They opposed, for example, the Pan Am hijacking in Karachi, and immediately after that incident they denied landing rights. They interceded with the TWA hijackers in Beirut. And of course three hostages once held in Lebanon by Islamic Jihad are today with their families here in the United States of America.

"When you are President, any American held captive against his will anywhere in the world is like your own son or daughter. I know that's the way our President feels about it. Yet you must also remain true to your principles. And I can tell you the President is absolutely convinced that he did not swap arms for hostages.

"The question remains of how the administration could violate its own policy of not selling arms to Iran. Simple hope explains it perhaps better than anything else. The President hoped that we could open a channel that would serve the interests of the United States and of our allies in a variety of ways. Call it leadership. Given 20-20 hindsight, call it a mistaken tactic if you want to. It was risky, but potentially of long-term value.

"The shaping of the Iranian policy involved difficult choices. As complex as the public debate on the issue would be, the matter was further clouded by the way in which the President's goals were executed, specifically allegations about certain activities of the National Security Council staff.

"As I have frequently said, mistakes were clearly made.

"Our policy of conducting a dialogue with Iran, which was legitimate and arguable, became entangled with the separate matter of an NSC investigation.

"The President learned of possible improprieties on a Monday. On Tuesday he disclosed the problem to the public and instructed the Attorney General to go forward with a full investigation. On Wednesday he created a bipartisan commission of outstanding individuals to review the role of the NSC staff and make recommendations for the future. And only days later he moved to have the court appoint an independent counsel to ensure a full accounting for any possible wrongdoing.

"The President pledged full cooperation with the United States Congress, urging it to consolidate and expedite its inquiries. He later named Frank Carlucci, a seasoned professional with broad experience and well-known to many people in Washington, to serve as his national security advisor. Now this was fast action in anybody's book.

"Those were actions I fully supported and which I believe the American people judged commendable.

"The President moved swiftly and strongly."

You've repeatedly said that your own private counsel to the President is confidential and that you'll never betray it.

Yet some stories are already out, stories that you had reservations about the Israeli involvement, and other accounts. Where did you stand? What was your role in all of this?

"I was aware of our Iran initiative and I supported the President's decision. I was not aware of and I would have opposed any diversion of funds, any ransom payments, or any circumvention of the will of the Congress or the law of the United States of America. As the various investigations proceeded, I said bluntly, 'Let the chips fall where they may.' We want the truth. The President wants it. I want it.

"If the truth hurts, so be it. We've got to take our lumps and move ahead.

"Politics don't matter. Personalities don't matter. Those who haven't served the President well don't matter. What matters is the United States of America."

What was the international fallout, the ramifications for our ongoing foreign policy, from all of this?

"First, we had to make certain that our foreign policy did not become paralyzed by distraction.

"There can be no denying that our credibility was damaged by this entire episode and its aftermath.

"We had a critical role to play internationally. We were trying to put U.S.-Soviet relations on a new footing, pursuing a breakthrough in arms reduction. We were working to end apartheid and create a more hopeful future for all Africans. We were solidifying the remarkable changes taking place in Asia, combating international terrorism in close conjunction with our allies, and fostering the development of democracy in Central America.

"We had to make certain that the freedom of the people in Central America was not held hostage to actions unrelated to them. This nation's support of those who are fighting for democracy in Nicaragua should stand on its own merits and not hang on events related to Iran. The Marxist-Leninist regime in Managua must not benefit from the errors of some people in Washington D. C.

"Our administration has a duty to follow a foreign policy that reflects the values of its citizens. This sounds simple, but it is often a very complex matter. It's not easy to translate general values into specific foreign policy programs. And this is why there is always so much internal debate over our nation's role in world affairs, from Iran to arms reduction."

Do you think Congress is getting in the way of an effective foreign policy?

"Foreign policy is a shared power. The founders of our country intended the legislative branch to participate with the executive branch in the broad formulation of foreign policy. But certainly that does not apply to the execution of that policy.

"Hamilton spoke in the Federalist Papers of the need to focus foreign policy in one man so that the nation could quickly and decisively and, if necessary, secretly achieve our goals abroad.

"John Marshall spoke of the President as 'the sole organ of the nation in its external relations, and its sole representative with foreign nations.' Some of the founders who later became President took an expansive view of the executive's powers when they were in office, often acting without consulting Congress.

"Nevertheless, Congress has in recent years enacted scores of statutes that regulate our foreign policy in the minutest detail."

The War Powers Act?

"That is one of the classic examples of such intrusion.

"In the past 200 years we have sent U.S. troops overseas more than 200 times without a declaration of war, each time to protect our national interests and national security. Should the need arise, any President should do so again without hesitation.

"Vermont Royster, editor emeritus of *The Wall Street Journal,* reviewed some of these executive actions and concluded that if the President had gone to Congress for authority to do what he did, the result would have been a long, hot, political battle. In some cases, even if the President had finally won Congressional approval, it would have been too late to make the action effective.

"In my view the War Powers Resolution is not only unwise but unconstitutional. We have limited the President's ability as Commander-in-Chief to respond flexibly when force is required, and we have restricted his actions without allowing for a Presidential veto.

"In the War Powers Resolution, Congress claims the power to act by concurrent resolution—that is, without Presidential approval. This the Supreme Court has already rejected as unconstitutional.

"These conflicts lead inevitably to efforts to drag the judiciary into foreign policy matters, where it least belongs. The recent lawsuit filed by 100 members of Congress, charging that the President's actions in the Persian Gulf violate the War Powers Resolution, is just one example. I don't believe the founders of our country envisioned any role for the judiciary beyond the adjudication of certain disputes that might arise under treaties."

Some say that the Executive branch needs to be brought under control, that such resolutions are necessary.

"Sometimes such restrictions get ridiculous: The Tunney and Clark amendments on Angola, the restrictions on arms exports, a requirement that our military bases over-seas use coal shipped from the United States no matter what the cost—there are many other examples.

"A bill passed by the Senate went so far as to prohibit any reduction in our consulates and missions abroad, and it earmarked funds for consulates in Salzburg, Strasbourg, Göteborg, Lyons, Düsseldorf, Tangier, Genoa, Nice, Pôrto Alegre, and Maracaibo.

"As Senator Danforth asked during debate on the bill, 'Does the role of the U.S. Senate in foreign policy extend to constantly tinkering with everything, fine-tuning every-thing?' He added, 'I would submit that no reasonable per-son anywhere in the world can predict how the United States stands on any foreign policy issue.'

"I don't think it's an exaggeration to say that it is getting as difficult to follow Congressional directives on foreign affairs."

No doubt the process makes it difficult to deal with the enemy?

"The potential for harm is obvious. In the midst of sensi-tive arms control negotiations, Congress considered amend-ments to legislate provisions of the SALT II treaty, a treaty that was proposed by a Democratic President and rejected by a Democratic Senate. It tried and is still trying to impose its own interpretation in the intelligence field.

"In Central America, the on-again, off-again effect of the Boland Amendment and other legislative actions has so tied up our support of the freedom fighters that our national resolve has remained in constant doubt.

"In effect we have been operating with a wobbly wheel in Nicaragua, conveying a sense of instability to all who observe us. I am concerned about what will happen after the Guatemala Peace Accord takes effect. Daniel Ortega is returning from Moscow for the event. He will boast of movement toward civil liberties in Nicaragua, and many in Congress will accept his claim.

"What we must resist in Nicaragua is a sham, an illusion of progress that takes the pressure off the Sandinistas, cripples the Contras, and strengthens the Communists' grip on power. We are engaged in the support of a courageous, patriotic people fighting for freedom against an openly Marxist-Leninist regime. We should not simply cut and run."

Yet that is exactly what may happen. It is the mood of Congress.

"The 1964 edition of the Congressional publication called *Legislation on Foreign Relations* was a single 650-page volume. By the middle of the '80s that had grown to three volumes of more than 1000 pages each. This is not policy-making or oversight. Often it is simply meddlesome make-work, intended to justify the growing staffs and budgets of proliferating subcommittees.

"In my view, turf warfare and competition for the camera contribute as much to the conflicts between the branches as politics and policy do."

So what's the solution?

"The challenge is to find a cooperative middle ground, one that respects the important constitutional role of the legislative branch and leaves the executive free to respond quickly and decisively to unforeseen circumstances and events.

"Toward that end, I called for creation of a Joint Intelligence Committee. It is a step recommended by the Administration's Task Force on Combatting Terrorism, which I chaired in 1985, and by the Tower Commission earlier this year. Such a committee would build mutual confidence, streamline the consultation process, reduce partisan tensions, and reduce leaks.

"I am encouraged by the strong bipartisan support shown for such a committee by members of the House, led by my good friend Henry Hyde and joined by Dante Fascell, Bill Broomfield, and 126 other cosponsors.

"Congressional reform should go further than a joint intelligence committee, however; it should also lead to greater consolidation of committee work touching on foreign policy.

"The initiative for such reforms ultimately must come from Congress itself, but I hope by my campaign for President to bring this issue to the forefront and speed the process along.

"As a nation we can deal most effectively with our adversaries if we are united. I hope to encourage a new spirit of bipartisanship on Capitol Hill, not just on matters of intelligence but in foreign policy generally. The President and Congress need to work together, and Congress needs to enact its own reforms. We *can* do better and we *must* do better because our national interest demands no less."

- 6 -
Hard Choices

After the Presidency of Lyndon Johnson, Presidential candidates in both parties routinely promised to go to war against an entrenched federal bureaucracy. The pledge to "get the government off our backs" helped elect Richard Nixon, Jimmy Carter, and Ronald Reagan.

By the time Reagan-Bush assumed office, four presidents (Gerald Ford included) had taken turns cutting fat from those mountains of regulations that singly appear imperative but in their totality are excessively oppressive. Most of the regulations that Nixon, Ford, and Carter had missed trimming were the ones written in stone or else protected by unchallenged presuppositions (or just money-heavy lobbies representing special interests).

President Reagan had given the job of deregulation to George Bush. Within one year those piles of regulations which govern our lives were cut in half. It was a great accomplishment. The Vice President was always quick to give the credit to fellow members of the Deregulatory Commission or to Senators, members of Congress, and their staffs, but the men and women in the Office of the Vice President knew the leadership that George Bush had shown, and there was a sense of pride for everybody on the team.

"The greatest reward comes from knowing that power has finally stopped flowing to Washington and has started flowing back to where it belongs—to the states. *The Christian Science Monitor* said recently, 'Decentralization of

81

power could be one of the most long-lasting effects of the Reagan Presidency.' I think that's right.

"We are experiencing the longest peacetime economic expansion in our history. Unemployment is down to 5.9 percent, with 13.7 million new jobs created in the past five years. Interest rates are down. Inflation is down and staying down. Personal income is up. Prosperity is widespread.

"But yes, there are still key concerns to be resolved, and they are serious. The budget and trade deficits remain far too large. To sustain prosperity and extend it to all Americans, we must remove these barriers to further economic growth."

In your speeches you keep talking about the disfranchised, those who haven't participated in the recovery. You've been criticized for that. Some say you sound like a Democrat.

"I care about people. Democrats don't have a monopoly on compassion.

"Make no mistake—I'm very proud of our recovery. I'm happy for the majority who are prospering as never before and for the poor who have been able to break out of the poverty cycle. But as long as there are hurting people out there, our job isn't over. As far as I'm concerned, we will never be a truly prosperous nation until all within it prosper.

"I want a prosperity that we can rely on. I want a prosperity that broadens, that deepens, and that touches all Americans, from the hollows of Kentucky to the oil fields of Oklahoma and Texas.

"We've got to continue to remove the barriers to growth. For seven years, steadily and surely, we have been lowering the unemployment rate. We must continue our pursuit of those three little words: jobs, jobs, and jobs.

"We've got to continue, and accelerate, our efforts to cut the federal budget deficit. There is much to be done in this area, an impasse to be broken. But I will not break it by breaking the people.

"There are those who say we must balance the budget on the backs of the workers and raise taxes again. But they are wrong. We should not raise taxes."

Mr. Vice President, just a little side step here. You've made some interesting comments on our tax code. Do you think tax reform has gone far enough?

"Government has a proper and legitimate role in the collection and dispersal of tax revenues. We must all pay our fair share. But for too long the rules of the game have been cloaked in deliberate ambiguity. The rules about what the IRS can do and about the taxpayer's rights are often unclear. I think it's time for a taxpayer's bill of rights, a bill of rights that spells out explicitly what the limits of IRS power are.

"I would put the force of my presidency behind this idea, one whose time has more than come.

"I want to add that I don't hate government. I'm proud of my long experience in government. I've met some of the best people in the world doing the people's business in the Congress and the agencies. A government that serves the people effectively and economically, and that remembers that the people are its master, is a good and needed thing."

The American farmers didn't seem to get in on the recovery, at least not until more recently.

"Rural America has been pretty severely tested in recent years. Hard times have driven people out of the country and into the city, shrinking the economies of the places they leave behind. In some of our small towns there is more plywood than plate glass downtown.

"For many people this has been a heartbreaking process. But the people who remain are survivors—self-reliant, optimistic, hardworking, and full of faith and generosity.

"All the indicators show that we've seen the bottom now and are headed back up. The economic news is encouraging. Personal income in Iowa, for example, is up almost 10 percent in the first three months of the year, compared to the same time last year. Even more heartening is the fact that construction income in the state has risen 20 percent, dramatic testimony that optimism is increasing and people are starting to look to the future."

What have we done? What's the difference?

"For one thing, there is evidence that the farm bill is beginning to work. Our more competitive prices, coupled with the drop in the dollar's value, have improved our ability to compete abroad. We are beginning to recover from the terrible hangover that followed the binge of the 70's, a binge of unsustainably high prices and land speculation caused by a cheap dollar and bad weather overseas.

"With our Conservation Reserve Program we have taken some of our most highly erodible farmland out of production for the next ten years, helping to preserve our soil and protect the environment.

"The administration also has proposed guaranteeing the borrowing stock of farmers who are members of the Farm Credit System. There have been problems with the credit system and changes need to be made, but in the meantime the interests of farmers must be protected.

"Making things better has been expensive. The cost of the U.S. farm program rose to 26 billion dollars in 1986, even more than the 22 billion spent by the European Common Market.

"But thanks to the farm bill, the farm program is providing stability and continuity in a field where the only constant is change."

America is still the breadbasket of the world.

"It's amazing. Our agricultural productivity is nothing short of miraculous. Three percent of our population is feeding the other 97 percent, and much of the rest of the world as well. This productivity allows us as consumers to spend an extremely small percentage of our disposable income on food.

"But at the same time, the competition is getting tougher every year. Technological advances being made in the laboratories, corn that resists insects, wheat that withstands drought, cows that produce more milk—all these will increase our agricultural output and, within the structure of the current farm program, may put further pressure on the farm economy."

Yet that must be good news for consumers?

"The problem is that for decades we have put our primary emphasis on increasing production. But increasing farmers' production does not necessarily increase farmers' profits. We should also concentrate on lowering the cost it takes to produce a bushel of corn."

Some suggest that it's time we use our agricultural advantage to leverage our way into a better trade position. Of course there would have to be more control.

"Some people want to respond to these challenges with a 'Can't do' philosophy that says, 'We give up.' Their policies of protectionism and production controls would result in trade barriers to our exports and mandatory acreage reductions that would cripple our farm economy. They must not be allowed to succeed.

"This 'Big Brother' approach to agriculture would have the government try to restrict production and raise prices by telling each farmer how many acres to plant. If government planners were that smart, the Soviets wouldn't have to depend on the West to feed their own people, and we wouldn't have billions of bushels of corn sitting in government storage.

"By raising and lowering output, mandatory controls would raise food prices for every consumer and would increase feed costs for livestock producers. Our crops would be less competitive overseas, and our export markets would evaporate.

"Rural America would be devastated. Everyone from the farm-implement-maker to the local fertilizer salesman would lose business. According to one estimate, more than two million jobs would be wiped out in industries related to farming.

"Of course, the export markets won't be there to lose if the trade bill now making its way through Congress is enacted. Its advocates want to duck the competition we face from abroad, in all sectors of the economy, by seeking protection from our rivals and demanding a share of foreign markets. The result is certain to be retaliation that will close, not open, markets to us.

"The question is, Can America compete?

"I believe it can, particularly in agriculture. I believe we can take our corn and beef abroad and increase our world market share, as long as we don't have to contend with the protectionist agricultural policies of Europe and Japan. But if the Democrats' trade bill passes, the very first victims will be our farmers."

What would you do?

"My approach is 180 degrees different. If we're so good at growing things, let's find new things to do with them.

"For example, researchers are trying to make biodegradable plastics from cornstarch. If they succeed, we could substitute corn for petroleum and improve our environment at the same time.

"That's pretty exciting, but it's still way off on the horizon. A practical step we can take today is to increase our use of alternative fuels.

"Detroit is ready now to make cars that would run on any combination of gasoline and alcohol, either ethanol (made from corn) or methanol (made from natural gas or coal or even wood). Imagine—grain alcohol and wood alcohol! Gasohol, which is 10 percent ethanol, is already widely available in the Midwest and can be used in any car on the road.

"Cars produce less pollution on alcohol fuels, and they perform better, too. The cars at the Indy 500 use straight methanol. Most of the gasoline in Germany and Austria contains methanol. And all the cars in Brazil run on either ethanol or ethanol-gasoline blend.

"The same arguments that made sense in Brazil make sense here, too. Use a surplus domestic resource—in their case, sugarcane; in our case, corn—to replace imported oil.

"What would that get us?

1) Less dependence on OPEC.
2) Cleaner air.
3) Improvement in our trade deficit.
4) Reduced corn surpluses.
5) Higher prices for farmers."

So much for the energy crisis.

"We've never had a true energy crisis in this country. We have an almost-unlimited ability to produce electricity from domestic resources like coal. What we had was an *oil* crisis, a shortage of fuels for transportation."

In the 1970's there was such panic over OPEC. There were predictions that our economy was about to collapse. The American lifestyle would change forever. Is there a real problem?

"There's no denying that OPEC held America hostage in the 1970's, and it threatens to do so again. Yet alternative fuels can set us free.

"In the short term we could establish a 'clean fuel standard' and require that fuel sold in areas that exceed federal standards for carbon monoxide contain at least 3 percent oxygen by weight. Ordinary gasohol, for example, would qualify.

"Colorado recently established an oxygen standard for some of its communities, including Denver, and both Phoenix and Albuquerque are considering similar action.

"Extended more wisely, such a requirement would create a demand for more than one billion bushels of corn, wheat, and potatoes. The market price of such crops would rise, and the government's storage and subsidy costs would fall.

"I might add that the State of California has been a national leader in going beyond that to encourage the use of straight methanol for environmental reasons."

It makes a lot of sense. One wonders why we haven't already put such programs into place.

"What sickens the American people about our farm program is not so much its enormous cost as the seeming wastefulness and pointlessness of it all. We pay farmers to produce crops that sit unwanted and unused, depressing prices in and of themselves.

"Greater use of ethanol offers us the chance to eliminate those surpluses and reduce our need for imported oil, while cutting costs to the federal government.

"The use of alternative fuels could also mean the development of a whole new generation of American cars. Automakers have spent the last 15 years trying to make cars lighter and more fuel-efficient. But fuel economy standards were enacted to reduce our dependence on oil. They should not constrain our use of alternative fuels such as methanol or ethanol. Cars could be made bigger, more powerful, and safer."

Do you think America has lost some of its confidence, that our Japanese and European trading partners have psyched us out? We've become followers instead of the trendsetters.

"We are just 12 years away from the year 2000. We need to have the imagination to dream great dreams. And energy independence is a great one. Imagine if we turn away from our dependence on imported oil! Domestic feedstocks, corn, natural gas, and coal will contribute to our fuel supply and help clean up our air. Then we start looking for energy not just from the Middle East but also from the U.S. Midwest.

"We need to have the courage and boldness to make the dream a reality. The farmer in the Midwest, the miner in Appalachia, and the driller in the oil patch all have a stake in such a dream.

"I've been talking about what I call 'the American solution' to the challenges of the 1990's. The American solution means facing up to foreign competition, not shrinking from it in fear. The American solution means competing through innovation, with alternative fuels. The American solution means looking to the future with the confidence that we can overcome the obstacles before us and with the determination to succeed."

Would you continue the price support system?

"I stand by the administration's attempt to phase out, over a reasonable period, those government subsidies that distort the agricultural market and restrict trade, but only if our trading partners do the same.

"These goals will not be achieved overnight, but they represent the direction in which we must go: freer markets, reduced governmental involvement, and expanded world trade."

How are some of our trading partners handling the changes in agriculture?

"Some are trying to see who can outsubsidize whom. In Japan the cost of food is kept so high by subsidies and tariffs that the Japanese spend 50 percent more for food than we do. I'm not worried about the ability of American farmers to compete in a country where steak costs 25 dollars a pound, if we can get access to the market.

"The American farmer doesn't want to remain dependent forever on government handouts; all he wants is a fair price from a free market, and we must continue to move toward that goal. But this doesn't mean that farmers should be thrown totally to the vagaries of the world market. Complete and sudden abandonment of the existing farm program would amount to unilateral economic disarmament, and it would create painful, wrenching havoc in rural America.

"Right now the farm program is like a plane that's way up in the air: If it just tries to stay aloft, it will run out of gas. But the answer is not simply to put the nose down and crash. The answer is to find a safe glide path for a landing.

"I believe there are three keys to that glide path: open markets abroad, new markets at home, and development of the rural economy."

And how are we going to get foreign markets to open up?

"There has to be hard-nosed negotiation, not mandatory retaliation and protectionism. We should devote an economic summit meeting to the subject of agriculture. I believe that our experience in dealing with the leaders of the free world—Thatcher, Kohl, Mitterand, and Nakasone—would greatly increase the chances of significant results from such a summit. Let me also say that I am opposed to agricultural embargoes. Food should not be used as a foreign policy weapon.

"But we should also concentrate on developing new markets for our farm products at home. I'm a tremendous believer in alcohol fuels not only because of aid to the farmers but also because of the enormous payoffs they bring in energy security and environmental quality. The administration's Task Force on Regulatory Relief, which I am proud to chair, has very actively cleared away bureaucratic obstacles to that development.

"Finally, we should emphasize development of the rural economy."

How would we do that?

"There are tremendous assets in rural America that haven't been adequately recognized and exploited. These include the skill and energy and dedication of the work force. If you're a businessman looking for the work ethic, you need look no farther than rural America.

"We should continue to expand our efforts to make rural areas more attractive to industry. Education is one answer—education for the future. For example, we should encourage our schools to make sure that no one graduates from high school without being able to use a computer.

"Why not provide retraining to farmers forced out of work by foreign competition? One way to do that would be to make worker-adjustment assistance available to farmers, as it is to factory workers.

"We could improve rural health care by ensuring that rural hospitals are treated fairly under federal health programs. We should consider restructuring federal assistance to rural areas in order to provide more flexibility to the states to fund their highest priorities. The Governors know far better than some bureaucrat in Washington what the needs of a local state are."

Lately, in some of your speeches, you've been talking about enterprise zones for rural areas, similar to the proposed plans for the inner cities.

"Why not? The tax breaks and other incentives would attract development to severely depressed rural communities."

Mr. Vice President, I'm from the Midwest, and in many areas there the economy is already diversifying.

"That's true. The continued strength of the U. S. economy is beginning to be felt, and it is bringing new opportunities and new hope to some of the areas that were hit the hardest.

"I believe the seeds have been sown for a new competitiveness in agriculture and a new vitality in America's heartland as we move into the 90's and the 21st century. But the 80's weren't easy on rural America. I want the children on the farms to be able to earn a decent living and raise their children where they themselves were raised.

"We are the greatest and most efficient producers of food that the world has ever known. Our future is limited only by our willingness to compete, to dare, and to dream."

Getting a good idea through Congress seems to be quite a chore. There are just so many constituencies and special interests. A bill is soon overloaded with costly amend-ments.

"Let me tell you a true story. A man who weighed 305 pounds wanted to lose weight in the worst way. So he went to the hospital to have an operation to have his stomach stapled. A surgeon implanted more than 70 tiny staples to constrict part of his stomach.

"Two days later the man walked down a hospital hall-way and spotted a refrigerator. Now he's suing the hospital for 250,000 dollars because he ate so much he popped his staples.

"Now doesn't that remind you of Congress?

"Here's a crowd that appropriates every dime the fed-eral government spends and runs 200-billion-dollar deficits in the midst of sustained economic growth. They go to the hospital for some Gramm-Rudman surgery, then they see a refrigerator filled with pork, and boom! There go the staples.

"How do you get these guys to stay on a diet?

"I'll tell you how. With a constitutional amendment requiring a balanced budget, and a line-item veto for the President. These are tools that almost every Governor in America needs."

Maybe the Democrats should be given another chance to help the farmers.

"What would the Democrats do? Their package of higher taxes and tariffs would do for the economy what Lizzie Borden did for her parents. Think back to 1980, when we had double-digit inflation, the prime rate at 21.5 percent, and a diagnosis of 'malaise.' This could come back again. You can be sure I won't raise taxes, and I won't start a trade war with our economic partners."

There are some in the Democratic Party who would tell you that the game is up, that American farmers can't compete with the rest of the world anymore. Their solution is to pull back inside fortress America, put up the protectionist walls of tariffs and trade barriers, and restrict your future to one of acreage reductions and subsidies and agricultural welfare.

"I reject that view categorically. I believe we *can* compete and *should* compete with the rest of the world. I believe that government should not be putting up trade barriers but tearing them down. I want our future to be one of free enterprise and competition and success in world markets. And I believe we have the ability to make it happen!

"Restrictive tariff legislation, the notorious Smoot-Hawley Act, helped bring on and worsen the Great Depression. We must not make the same mistake twice.

"We must enforce our trade laws vigorously against those countries which refuse to let American products compete on an equal basis in a free market. But a restrictive trade policy will lead to retaliation abroad, and the first people who will be hurt are farmers."

This brings us back to the deficits. Do you blame it all on the Democrats? They would lay it at the feet of Ronald Reagan.

"Sometimes we get carried away casting the blame, and that goes for me too. But it seems to me that this is a good time for Democrats and Republicans in the Congress to work with the President to reduce these deficits. If there was anything good that came from the market volatility last fall, it just might have been the beginning of a cooperative effort on these problems.

"It doesn't matter where the fault lies. This is not a time for Democrats to be pointing the finger at us. This is a time for our two great parties to join together and do something good and positive for our people, our country, and the world. "I want to see stable markets, devoid of radical swings. Free markets, free to seek their own levels. Open markets, markets that are regulated to protect against fluctuation. This might mean new rules, such as a limit on the price swings permitted on a given day in the futures market.

"The role of the executive branch is to keep the underlying economy strong, give the people the facts, and work with Congress on the budget deficit and the trade deficit. The role of Congress is to get on with its work in getting the budget deficit down, while resisting the impulse to enact protectionist trade barriers."

If you were President, are there any programs that you would increase? What are your priorities?

"Education, for one. All our hopes for our children will mean little if we don't make sure that the education they're given is outstanding. The founders knew this. Two hundred years ago they used to say, 'To plan for a decade, plant a tree, but to plan for a century, teach the children.'

"We have made improvements. I take great pride in the fact that our administration has been at the forefront of the educational reform movement—but it's not enough. The younger, hungrier nations are passing us by, and we've got to compete and surpass them. It is one of my priorities and one of the critical issues facing us in the years ahead.

"And then there's the environment. There are two things that we pass on from generation to generation without even speaking of our pride or their preciousness.

"One is the treasure of our minds and hearts. The other is the treasure of our land—the environment, the terrain. I don't think we've done enough to protect it these past dozen years or so. I don't think we've given the land its due.

"Sooner or later we're going to pay the price of our distraction, unless we act now and recommit ourselves to protecting the land we love."

Why education? How did this become such a great priority for you?

"One thing is already clear about the 90's. As a nation we will face an unprecedented level of competition—not just militarily, from our traditional adversaries, but also economically, from our friends and allies.

"More than 2200 years ago Aristotle wrote that the fate of empires depends on the education of youth. His words are just as true today. If we are to prevail against our global competition, we must be adequately prepared.

"Just as important, education represents a proven pathway to a better life. For generations of immigrants fleeing poverty and persecution in Europe, Asia, and Latin America, the education of their children was the focus of their lives and the purpose of their personal sacrifice.

"Universal access to public education is most fundamentally an expression of our deeply shared commitment to opportunity for all. It showcases our view that individual merit will prevail if given an equal chance."

But does education really make a difference? One hears stories of high school dropouts becoming millionaires and graduates with doctorate degrees looking for work.

"Of course education isn't enough by itself, but there is overwhelming evidence that it is the great lifting mechanism of an egalitarian society. *It works.* People who earn a high school degree are only one-third as likely to be poor as those who drop out. The surest way to win the war against poverty is to win the battle against ignorance. Our greatest President was born in a log cabin, but he walked to school and raised himself up to greatness.

"The challenge of the past has been to break down the barriers to that opportunity. It is a task that is not yet finished. But the challenge of the future is not just to make education more available, but to make it more worthwhile.

"We have succeeded in broadening the base. More of our citizens are educated now than in any previous generation. But the quality of the education has suffered.

"In the 60's and 70's we were paying out more and enjoying it less. The amount of money we spent on each student's education doubled in constant dollars. The average class size shrank, and the percentage of teachers with master's degrees doubled. Yet national SAT scores fell by 85 points.

"The way it is now, even though we spend more on education than any other nation on Earth, we just don't measure up. On an algebra test given to twelfth-graders around the world, we came in fourteenth out of fifteen countries, just ahead of Thailand and just behind Hungary! On a test given to our 12-year-olds, 20 percent were unable to locate the United States on a world map!

"Some 13 percent of our 17-year-olds are functionally illiterate. This means that they lack the reading skills they need to live and work."

The Democrats would blame Reaganomics and cuts in funding.

"Money is an easy answer to these problems, but it is not the fundamental answer, and it has not paid off. The federal role in education is limited, and that's the way it should be. The primary governmental role has always belonged to local school boards and to an increasing degree the states. The fundamental answer is to make better use of what we have.

"We can't succeed if the children spend seven or eight minutes a day reading silently in class and two hours a day watching television.

"We can't succeed if academic bureaucrats impose a value-free homogenized curriculum in the classroom while drugs and violence flourish in the halls.

"We can't succeed if teachers don't assign, parents don't supervise, and students don't complete more homework.

"Homework pays. Educational achievement has less to do with money or class size than it does with homework assigned and completed. Low-ability students who do just one to three hours of homework a week, half an hour a night, perform as well as average-ability students who do none at all.

"That's just common sense. But in some educational circles, common sense has not been the common wisdom. One-third of our nine-year-olds and more than a fifth of our 17-year-olds say they have no homework assigned on a typical day.

"Hard work, a respect for learning, and self-discipline— these qualities are not just *how* you learn in school, but they're also *what* you learn in school. They are the values that lead to success.

"As Alfred North Whitehead said, 'Education is discipline for the adventure of life.' What makes us good workers also makes us good parents, citizens, and neighbors."

But can values really be taught? Some say that the teaching of moral values is only a smokescreen for getting religion back into the schools.

"I don't buy that. I think most of us know what constitutes good character. It includes such qualities as decency and fairness, honesty and tolerance, self-discipline and respect for law. Sadly, not everyone learns these values in their home or church. The schools must play a role too. We should teach our children what I call the four R's: reading, writing, 'rithmetic, and respect.

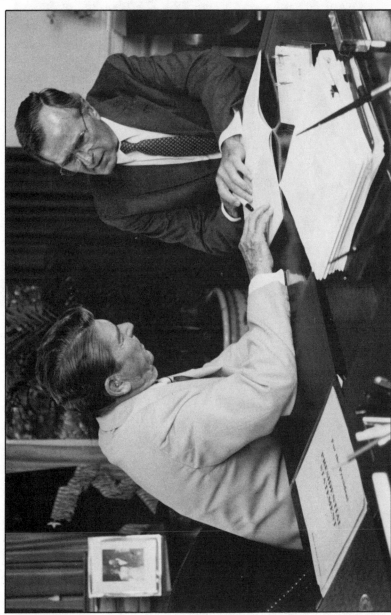

Dave Valdez, The White House

On President Reagan: "Seven years ago a nation that needed to trust again turned to him and rediscovered its spirit. I am proud to have been his partner . . . a part of his great work."

Dave Valdez, The White House

"There are two things that we pass on from generation to generation . . . one is the treasure of our minds and hearts. The other is the treasure of our land—the environment."

"Martin Luther King once said, 'We must remember that intelligence is not enough. Intelligence plus character is the goal of true education.'

"It's wrong for us to exclude the role of our faith and religion from our school textbooks. We need to teach our youth the truth about the Pilgrims and how our country was born in a search for religious tolerance. We need to teach them why we are one of the few nations to celebrate a thanksgiving and just who it is that we have been thankful to all these years."

Exactly what do you think it will take to turn the situation around?

"First, we should demand more from students—higher academic standards, with more emphasis on core courses such as English, math, science, and history. There should be more homework. We should test students, early and often, to make sure they're learning what they should. We should put a stop to automatic promotion and graduation. Every student ought to be able to operate a computer before graduation.

"Right now, only one federal program measures student achievement on a regular basis: the National Assessment of Education Progress. For a small amount of additional money we can test on more subjects and compile state-by-state data for the first time.

"Second, we should demand more from teachers. To raise the quality in the classroom, we should have competency tests for beginning teachers in the subject they teach and in the proper use of the English language. At the same time we should break down the barriers to talented people who want to teach and who have demonstrated their competence in other fields.

"Third, we should demand more from school administrators—more leadership, less red tape in the classroom, and less drugs and violence in the halls. I've met with some of our experts on education, and they've all made one very important point: Where you have a good, strong principal, you have a good school.

"Fourth, we should demand more from parents—more involvement in the home, in shutting off the television and getting their kids to read. We cannot succeed if children spend seven to eight minutes a day reading silently in class and 130 minutes a day watching television at home.

"Finally, we should demand more from the businesses in our communities—more partnerships with local schools, including commitments to help train high school students for jobs after they graduate. We should encourage innovative programs for inner-city youth, like Eugene Lang's guarantee of college tuition for those who graduate from high school."

Do you envision increased federal aid?

"We may need to change or restructure our aid program, but it involves more than throwing money at a problem. We could provide more choices for parents and students— for example, within the public school system. This includes schools of excellence for exceptional students in science and math.

"We should be providing merit pay and special recognition to reward good teachers. The vast majority are good and dedicated teachers who really love their kids and their profession. Let me tell you, I am for teachers! Let's give them the support they need to control their classrooms and concentrate on teaching.

"Finally, we should be providing more assistance to the disadvantaged. In their early years they can be helped with the Head Start Program and in remediation, particularly in literacy. Not everyone has a caring parent, but everyone needs a teacher or advisor who cares about him,

who knows his name, who hurts when it hurts. If we provide special attention to those with special needs, we can wipe out illiteracy the way we wiped out polio. Every kid should be able to read and speak English.

"The important thing is that in demanding more academic performance we are providing more opportunity to all students, particularly to those who have the farthest to go. The poor are not served by meaningless diplomas. They are served by real preparation for the demands of real life."

You've proposed a "college bond" program or a special tax break for college savings.

"In higher education today the question is just as much *access* as it is *quality*. And I mean by that *economic* access.

"Many middle-class families are panicked by the high costs of four years of college, the specter of 100,000 dollars per child. Such figures may be exaggerated by projections of inflation, but as parents plan for the future, image is as important as reality if fears of economic hardship deter bright and able students.

"According to one recent survey, 77 percent of all Americans believe tuitions are rising so fast that a college education will soon be out of the average family's reach. What view of the future will they share at night with their kids?

"I believe a college education should be financed in three stages: with money saved by parents before the college· years, with work and student aid during college, and with loans to be paid off after graduation.

"Right now, on the average, students pay one-third of their college bill themselves, from their own savings and employment income. More than half of all full-time undergraduates hold jobs during the academic year.

"And for middle- and low-income students, at public and private colleges alike, the aid package often includes a 2,500-dollar loan. Over four years that's 10,000 dollars in potential indebtedness.

"What's missing from this picture is savings. Too few Americans are saving for their children's education in the years before college. Only 40 percent of high school seniors surveyed said their families had put away anything for college costs.

"I think parents should start saving years in advance in order to spread the burden over a longer period and to make a larger contribution. That's why I favor the creation of a College Savings Bond."

How would it work?

"It would work just as the U.S. Savings Bonds do now, except that their income would be tax-free if applied to college tuition. With a payroll deduction of as little as 25 dollars per month, a parent could fund a child's tuition at a state college or university. And 140 dollars a month would be enough for tuition at an independent college or university.

"Such a program would address only part of the problem, however. Economic access to college would remain a hurdle for those who lack the ability to save any amount at all. For such families, I would support additional help at the federal level, continued funding of the college Work-Study program, expansion of the income-contingent loan program, and continuation of grants for low-income students."

You've been the champion deregulator and you've made it pretty clear that you want to cut back on federal spending, but your educational program seems to be an exception.

"That's because I believe we will spend the money one way or another way. Why spend it building prisons when, in some cases, education will reduce antisocial behavior? Why merely give money to the poor if they really want education and an opportunity to work?

"Earlier this year I attended the national finals of the 'Mathcounts' competition for seventh- and eighth-graders. There were more than 200 students from every state. Talk about smart! Those kids were solving complex problems before the entire question was read!

"The question which won it for Russell Mann of Tennessee was this: 'It takes 20 square tiles, each with 3-foot sides, to cover a certain floor. How many square tiles, each with 9-inch sides, will it take to cover the floor?'

"As I watched those eager hands shoot into the air, I stood in awe of what those young students had accomplished.

"Seeing those kids and so many others, as Barbara and I travel, convinces me that in the years ahead education can be our most powerful economic program, our most important trade program, our most effective urban program, our best program for producing jobs and bringing people out of poverty. The best investment we can make is in our children.

"H. G. Wells wrote, 'Civilization is a race between education and catastrophe.' We must not let the latter triumph."

Let's talk about the space program. We're obviously having some problems. Is this an area where we will be cutting back? Have we lost our sense of adventure? Is it too expensive, at least for the moment, to keep pressing?

"After the space shuttle tragedy, when the President asked me to go to the Cape to express condolences to the families, I saw another source of their strength. In her time of sorrow, only hours after the tragedy, Dick Scobee's wife, June, stood up and said, 'Before you came here we all talked about it: The program must go forward. We don't want our loved ones to have died in vain.'

"I've often been to Cape Canaveral, and as you might expect of someone from Houston, to the Johnson Space

Center as well. I always find these installations impressive and exciting. The people there are working on the frontiers of human imagination, making dreams into reality.

"How can we give up on our dreams?

"Our nation's capital in Washington is blessed with the superb resources of the Smithsonian Institution, great museums of the world devoted to American history, to natural history, and to the art of all nations, but the enthusiasm shown for the Air and Space Museum far outstrips all the others. People, young and old, from America and around the world pour into that enormous structure to gaze skyward and see the vehicles that carried the pioneers of flights.

"In very basic ways our exploration of space defines us as a people. It shows our willingness to take great risks for great rewards, to challenge the unknown, to reach beyond ourselves, to strive for knowledge and innovation and growth. Our commitment to leadership in space is symbolic of the role we seek in the world."

What have we really learned, in a practical sense, from our space exploration?

"We've actually learned more about earth than about space. Thirty years have passed since Sputnik. Suddenly we can see planet Earth as it is: a tiny grain of sand in the vastness of space, a shining sphere in the infinite darkness.

"I recall the old fisherman's prayer, 'The sea is so large, Lord, and my boat is so small.' We're all fellow passengers in this boat called Earth. We should be bold and venture seaward, but we must also make sure our boat is in good repair. The space program can play a role in doing both.

"For example, it's becoming ever more obvious that man's activity on the planet is having a significant and possibly irreversible effect on our environment, not just locally but globally.

"The hole in the ozone layer observed over the Antarctic, attributed to the use of chlorofluorocarbons, portends significant increases in skin cancer rates. And our reliance on fossil fuels and the consequent warming of the Earth through the 'greenhouse effect' could have radical implications for the future of agriculture in the United States and the world.

"A hotter and dryer Midwest could go from breadbasket to basket case. The advancing deserts, particularly in Africa, could make large food-producing areas uninhabitable. Important variations in vegetation covers and in coastlines have already been observed with existing measurement capabilities.

"We face the prospect of being trapped on a boat we have irreparably damaged, not by the cataclysm of war but by the slow neglect of a vessel we believed to be impervious to our abuse.

"Nature was once the great enemy of man, a ferocious and fearful force to be conquered, tamed, and harnessed to our needs. Now we find that we must protect her from ourselves. Walt Kelly was talking about pollution when he penned the immortal words, 'We have met the enemy, and he is us.'

"I'm for using the great energy and excitement of our expeditions into space to look back, to discover what it is we are doing to our Earth, and to alter our self-destructive course. Why not use our dreams to help us find solutions?"

And how would we do this?

"I like some of Dr. Sally Ride's ideas. Earlier this year she delivered a report to NASA in which she outlined four reasonable options for the space program. The first she called 'Mission to Planet Earth.'

"Such a mission would create a global observational system in space, aimed at developing a fundamental understanding of the Earth system, in order to predict changes that might occur either naturally or as a result of human activity.

"Dr. Ride explained that a mission to Earth was not the kind of major program which the public normally associates with an agency famous for Apollo, Viking, and Voyager. But she wrote, 'This initiative is a great one, not because it offers tremendous excitement and adventure, but because of its fundamental importance to humanity's future on this planet.'

"We have to remember, as we chase our dreams into the stars, that our first responsibility is to our Earth, to our children, to ourselves. Yes, let's dream, and let's pursue those dreams, but let's first preserve the fragile and precious world we inhabit.

"I've talked about my great concern about the cost of government and the size of the federal budget deficit. We can't write a blank check to NASA or any other federal agency. While our dreams are unlimited, our resources are not, and we must choose realistic missions that recognize those constraints."

What would you do specifically if you were calling the shots?

"I would create a National Space Council, chaired by the Vice President and composed of the heads of such departments as Commerce, Defense, State, and Transportation in addition to NASA. Our space effort must incorporate elements not only of pure science and exploration but also of national security and economic growth. There needs to be a comprehensive strategy for space.

"NASA should remain the lead agency in exploring the frontiers of space science and technology, from development of a transatmospheric vehicle to construction of a space station. What it should *not* be is a freight service for routine commercial payloads.

"That should be the province of the private sector, and we have already taken first steps in that direction by requiring the use of civilian launch services. But the government procurement process is a model of suffocating bureaucratic excess.

"A launch proposal submitted by General Dynamics took 4000 pages! A similar proposal to launch a European satellite required only 165 pages. Clearly we can take steps to streamline efficiency.

"We need to compete with the Soviets, the Europeans, and even the Chinese in reaching low-earth orbit. The Ride Report said this: 'A space program that can't get to orbit has all the effectiveness of a navy that can't get to sea.'

"The Soviets, with 91 launches last year, are now offering to launch our satellites for us. They say they will soon sell Earth photos with resolution as fine as six meters—five times better than the U. S. Landsat."

We're locked in, aren't we? There's really no alternative but going on with the shuttle.

"In the short term we have to reconstruct the replacement shuttle. But because Mission to Planet Earth would require the ability to launch large payloads, it would justify the building of a heavy-lift launch vehicle, designed for minimum weight.

"Such a vehicle should deliver a pound of payload for a small fraction of the cost of the space shuttle.

"The Soviets mass-produce such vehicles and launch them routinely. We need them too. We particularly need them for SDI. Any space-based defense will require a deep reduction in the price of placing cargo in orbit in order to be affordable. Costs need to be cut by a factor of ten."

Are you committed to SDI? There is debate about its cost or even whether it will work.

"I'm committed to a vigorous SDI program. The Soviets have been working on strategic defenses much longer and harder than we have—in fact, well before my time at the CIA in the mid-70's.

"They don't like the fact that the United States has an SDI research program of its own. They want to keep a monopoly on strategic defense, and they have made a major effort to accomplish that goal at the negotiating table. But they will not succeed.

"Mission to Planet Earth, a strong civilian launching program, and strategic defense—these are important immediate goals. But we must also dream great dreams. We must also look outward and reach toward the stars.

"As a nation we owe our standing in the world as much to our brains as to our brawn. Yet we have no monopoly on intellectual initiative. To maintain our advantage, we must aggressively advance the frontiers of our knowledge.

"Remember, our leadership in space has provided direct payoffs in technological and economic progress. By forcing ourselves to reach demanding goals, we have reached the rewards of breakthroughs that resulted.

"We should make a long-term commitment to manned and unmanned exploration of the solar system. There is much to be done. Future exploration of the moon, a mission to Mars, probes of the outer planets. These are worthwhile objectives, and they should not be neglected. They should be pursued in a spirit of bipartisanship and international teamwork.

"In the defense of our country or in the interest of economic growth, we must compete with the other spacefaring nations. But the expansion of our frontiers to the far reaches of the solar system should be a matter for cooperation among the peoples of the world, for ultimately we voyage outward not as Americans or Soviets, French or Japanese, but as humans.

"The signing of a five-year agreement with the Soviet Union to cooperate in the exploration of outer space for peaceful purposes is the first step in this direction.

"International cooperation is also critical to the success of Mission to Planet Earth. Fortunately, the concept is supported by several international organizations and may emerge as a theme for International Space 1992.

"As a nation, we've got to continue on the path that we've blazed, to discover and examine what lies beyond Earth. The exploration of space provides our children, the next generation of scientists and engineers, with a vision that ignites their energies and imagination.

"With faith in the future and a renewed sense of commitment, we can regain the spirit of Mercury and Apollo. The question for Americans, a people of pioneers, will never be 'Should we explore the universes?' but 'How can we not?' "

It's all pretty complex, Mr. Vice President. I'll admit playing armchair quarterback from time to time, and sometimes the solutions seem simple. We are still a young country, and Vietnam notwithstanding, we are still rather optimistic or naive. We want to do it all.

"We face some pretty difficult challenges in the years ahead, but the word 'challenge' is just another word for *opportunity*. If we seize those opportunities we can lead America into a new era of peace and prosperity.

"We live in the freest, the fairest, the most generous nation on the face of the earth. Faith in America? The vast majority of the people have it. I'll always defend this great land. I plan to help lead it, and help it spread the light of freedom. I will never apologize for America. The idea is just as good as it was 200 years ago."

George and Barbara Bush. "It was one of those storybook marriages. Forty-three years later they are still in love."—George Bush Jr.

- 7 -
Family Comes First

It is impossible to fully understand the Vice President outside the context of his own family. There is an electricity, a special magic, when Barbara and the children are nearby.

When all four boys recently appeared with their father on a morning television talk-show, the telephone lines lit up for hours. Some said that they were reminded of the Kennedys, that they had never seen so many young men in the same family so bright and handsome and personable.

As one would expect of a couple who has been married more than 40 years, the Vice President and his wife have become very bonded. There is the sense that they are both very much at peace with themselves and extraordinarily self-assured. They find it easy to offer compliments to others, and they notice little things that the more self-conscious and self-important people wouldn't see. Both are very bright, with a keen sense of humor. If there is a difference, it is that Barbara's mischievous wit is more public. And then there is her extraordinary imagination. A simple encounter with Barbara Bush in a receiving line may very well end up as a good story to tell. When Barbara considered doing a book about the George Bush family, she ended up writing the autobiography of C. Fred Bush, the family story told through the eyes of their cocker spaniel.

There is no doubt that George Bush is the leader of his household. To hear it from the children, his slightest rebuke reverberates like thunder to their ears. They still hold him in great respect.

111

In that sense Barbara is the great equalizer. If the Vice President is deliberate, she is spontaneous.

She is always there on Air Force Two or at the residence in the afternoons, working her needlepoint while the Vice President, sitting nearby, has a dozen staffers ranged around him giving their reports. When there is a contradiction or someone misspeaks, she will look up, raise her eyebrows, and give someone in the circle an "insider's knowing look," her eyes twinkling, already formulating what fun she will have with it later.

If one tried to compare her to a recent first lady or other prominent woman in public life, they might think of Betty Ford, in that Barbara is very practical about what she believes and is very frank. But truly there is no public personality with which to compare her. I would reduce it to one sentence: Barbara Bush is fun to be around. But that too can be deceptive. Her charm makes her a formidable advocate for her very serious views. Some issues she keeps to herself. If the Vice President is discreet in his relationship with President Reagan and the advice he offers, then so is Barbara Bush in her own relationship with her husband.

Barbara Bush: "When I disagree with him, George and I talk about it. It is *never* public."

There is one other very prominent characteristic of the Bush family: They are friendly—all of them. The list of "friends of the family" is itself quite a network and probably numbers into the thousands.

The interesting thing is that all of this began before the Vice President's political career. A cynical political observer may decry that fact, but it is true. During their married years in the Navy, the Bush apartment was the place to be. In West Texas, friends were always stopping by for barbecued hamburgers in the backyard. Today, Secret

Service restrictions notwithstanding, the atmosphere is just as amicable. The children, like the parents, are always reaching out to bring new friends into the warmth of that family circle.

In fact, perhaps the only rule of good management which the Vice President violates is the admonition that management should not be friends with the employees. Every new staffer quickly grows to love the family, and this is precisely because the family takes the time to know them as human beings.

Barbara: "George Bush looks for the best in everybody. He doesn't question motives."

I will never forget one special night during an early swing through the South. At the spur of the moment I suddenly found myself invited to dinner with the Bush family. The Vice President explained that it meant tagging along to an informal afternoon event but promised a great evening. "And you can't wear that," he said, referring to my dark blue suit. He promptly gave me one of his own golf shirts.

As it turned out, dinner was at Walt Disney's Epcot Center. After typically arriving via service roads and back entrances, the Vice President and entourage suddenly appeared in the heart of Disney World.

Tourists on the streets of Epcot's Chinatown were startled. A group standing in line for some event broke into delightful smiles, excited exclamations, and finally a rousing applause as we disappeared into the Chinese restaurant.

The Vice President, Mrs. Bush, Deputy Chief of Staff David Bates, and myself sat at one table. The Secret Service took several tables around us.

It was a delightful evening talking about China politics, and everybody's favorite books. Having lived in the People's Republic (serving there as one of America's first representatives), the Bushes could rattle off the names of some dishes that were new to David and me.

When the food arrived we were soon trading dishes and declaring our personal favorites in that grand tradition of Americans eating Chinese food. The conversation was so captivating that we hardly noticed Disney's grand-finale laser-fireworks display over the lake outside.

The evening was evidently my initiation into that greater Bush family, and as someone new to the circle it was deeply meaningful.

Of course, when this book project was launched, I tried to think back to the informal conversations that had taken place on the road and at the residence. I knew that no picture of George Bush would be complete without somehow capturing that sense of family that could someday embrace the nation.

"I'm pleased by what I would describe as an overdue resurgence of traditional values that derive from our broad Judeo-Christian heritage. They are not overtly religious. In some cases they could simply be called 'common sense,' or 'what works.'

"We have engaged in a lot of social experimentation over the last 25 years, but the fact is that much of it, from permissiveness to promiscuity, from open classrooms to open marriages, just hasn't worked. Much of it has been destructive to our family structure.

"Family is not a neutral word for me; it's a powerful word, full of emotional resonance. I was part of a strong family growing up, and I have been fortunate to have a strong family grow up around me.

"I have had many great and exciting moments in my life, but I can say without equivocation that my family has been the source of my greatest joys, from the deep satisfaction of having provided for my children, of seeing them grow up and marry and have families of their own, to the simple pleasures of grandchildren bouncing on our bed before breakfast.

"I believe that we lost sight of these basic yet profound human pleasures in the 60's and 70's. The ideas of marriage and lifelong commitment were labeled passé and old-fashioned."

And why this resurgence?

"Perhaps in part because of the fear of AIDS, and more importantly because the alternatives proved to be such tragic dead-ends.

"There's a reason why the sanctity of marriage is a central part of religious faith, and it isn't because of superstition, and it isn't because of a plot to enslave women. It's because it *works*.

"A good marriage can be hard going sometimes, and nothing like the romantic ideals that the young may hope for and expect. But sticking with it through the rough spots can yield a stronger, richer, deeper relationship, with stronger, richer, deeper personal rewards. Barbara and I have now celebrated 43 years together.

"The spread of AIDS is a terrible calamity for this country and the world, the full dimensions of which we can only guess at. But if this black cloud of pain and death has any silver lining, it is that people are thinking more seriously about what it means to make or break a commitment to each other."

There has been a national discussion on the breakup of the American family. But what can be done? Does government really have a role?

"Government can provide leadership from what Teddy Roosevelt called 'the bully pulpit,' and we can do a little more.

"Social attitudes will always be much more powerful than government policies. But at the margins, government can act in a positive way to help the family.

"For example, we should provide welfare benefits that keep families together, not split them apart. The current system is a disgrace.

"Second, we should enforce the responsibilities that fathers have for the families they create. It is a mockery of justice that fathers can avoid making child support payments ordered by the courts. We should go after them hard.

"Third, we should do everything we can to stop the tragic number of abortions taking place every day, every week, every month. We must stand up for life.

"Finally, we should encourage the alternative of adoption. More than 140,000 children are adopted each year, but thousands of childless families are still waiting for children to adopt. At the same time, many thousands of children with special needs, such as those with physical, mental, or legal handicaps, are not adopted.

"My own son Marvin is an adoptive parent, and I know how complicated and discouraging the process is. We should look for ways to make adoption easier for families who want children, and we should encourage women who face an unwanted pregnancy to choose life—adoption—over death."

In 1986 I was given the title of Liaison for Coalitions to the George Bush Committee and began reporting directly to G. W. Bush, the eldest son of the Vice President. For many years he had been called George, Jr., so much so that long ago he had resigned himself to the situation. Actually, the Vice President's name is George Herbert Walker Bush, making his son George Walker unique in name as well as in personality.

If one were to track his career on paper, one might conclude that George W. was the perfect understudy for his father. He had followed those footsteps into the oil business in West Texas, and after graduating from Yale he had entered the service, where he flew F-102's. In 1987 the 41-year-old businessman was already being promoted by some as a future Governor of Texas. Ironically, his father's own political career may have interrupted those plans. In politics, no skill or resource is more important than loyalty, and George W.'s presence in Washington was needed. In a reversal of his father, who had packed his bags and headed West, George W. had taken his wife, Laura, and beautiful twin daughters and headed East.

He was an easy man for which to work, with a quick mind that could grasp a complex situation and make a decision. His presence was immediately felt at the committee. Sometimes when I proposed a project, he so quickly digested the details that I wondered if he had really understood. But only days later I would hear him explaining it all to someone else, and sometimes he would probe me for details of which I thought he was hardly aware.

This book project was one of those "details." From time to time he would ask how things were going, and I would tell him what I needed. George arranged interviews with other family members, and in between those hectic hours of campaign work he himself would sometimes talk about the Vice President and what it was like growing up in the George Bush family.

G.W.B.: "Our home was one of discipline and love—love first and discipline second. George Bush set standards. Respect your elders, be polite, be forgiving, be trustworthy, and above all, be honest. If any of us ever violated the basics of love, he was quick to point it out to us, not in a mean way but in a loving and forgiving way.

"I'll never forget the day when, as a young man, I walked out on a job. I had agreed to work for a certain amount of time and later decided that it was time for me to go."

Was this for your father or someone else?

G.W.B.: "You never worked for him—this campaign is an extraordinary exception. George Bush did not believe in nepotism. His view was that each of his offspring should receive the best education possible and then go out and make his own way in life.

"Anyway, I had agreed to work for this company a certain amount of time. It was a summer job, but a week prior to the deadline I decided to leave.

"Well, my father found out about it. Follow-through and commitment were among the things he strongly believed in. So I was called into his office in Houston. He looked at me and said, 'Son, you agreed to work a certain amount of time and you didn't. I just want you to know that you have disappointed me.'

"Those were the sternest words to me, even though he said them in a very calm way. He wasn't screaming and he wasn't angry, but he was disappointed. When you love a person and he loves you, those are the harshest words someone can utter.

"I left that office realizing I had made a mistake. About two hours later I got a phone call from him. He was inviting me to go with him to a Houston Astros game.

"He is a man of strong principles, but a very forgiving man as well. He has never held a grudge against his kids. He has never been the type of person to put our failures in the context of his life and all that he has achieved. It's our failures in the context of our *own* lives. And by this I also mean that he is never one to say, 'Well, I look bad now as a result of your behavior.' It's always, 'You need to improve yourself.' He's been a great father from that standpoint."

Marvin Bush: "I think what made for a great family experience was that there was always a feeling of warmth. When I came into the house I felt that. I knew I was surrounded by people who loved me. At first I really wasn't that aware of it; I thought everyone else had the same situation. But when I started bringing friends home, I realized that we had something special.

"Of course I was a little younger, and a little more sensitive about being teased, so I thought I was getting a raw deal. But later I realized that this was as much as anything an expression of my siblings' love toward me or my parents' love toward me. And so I think the feeling of warmth and camaraderie was what characterized our house."

Neil Bush: "I had a reading problem. I did okay if it was a book about baseball. But if it wasn't a subject I was really interested in, it would be just too difficult for me to read. Mom hauled me all over to reading specialists. Both Mom and Dad gave me continuous support. They never discouraged me. They were always reinforcing and encouraging whatever good I did. When I talk to people about my Dad now, I say, 'If I can ever be measured one-half the father he has been, my life will have been a huge success.' "

G.W.B.: "We really live for those times when we're together in Maine. It's the focal point of our whole family. Maine is a beautiful setting; it's one of God's really great creations. But for us it's more than that—it's symbolic of family, a place filled with memories. It's an anchor in the storm, a place where we can all come to be with each other.

"Every morning at 6:00 or 6:30, the sun comes up across the Atlantic and blazes in the windows. The little kids, full of excitement for the day's adventures ahead, pop out of their beds. These are children ranging from one to ten. Sometimes they wake up their parents, and downstairs they run. They immediately run to their grandmother and grandfather's bed. And the scene is one of utter family joy.

"The classic morning scene, the one in the movies, shows a grumpy Mom and Dad yelling at the kids, not wanting to face the day. Not George and Barbara Bush. Their little grandkids come running into their room one at a time, piling onto the bed, playing with the toys they've got scattered around their bedroom for them. In another room there are a couple of parents reading the newspaper with a cup of coffee.

"It is a scene that I wish everyone could see, because it is a scene of love and family togetherness. And that happens every morning; it's how we start our mornings. To me it is so symbolic of the respect our family has for George and Barbara Bush. They have really been an example."

Marvin: "There aren't a lot of family stories about Mom and Dad's courtship. I think we all just sort of assumed that they were always a couple, that they grew up in the same house.

"It was really love at first sight. It seems that my Dad was zonked over the head by this outgoing, charming woman, and just like everything else he's done in his life, he decided that she was the one he was going to marry, and so he did. I guess they met in high school and then he was off to the war."

He had her name on his plane.

Marvin: "Yes, I saw a picture of that. Obviously this romance was already on during their high school years."

G.W.B.: "As I understand the story, of course, since I wasn't there, but I'm told it was love at first sight. I think Mother had heard of George Bush's reputation from a near-by city and Dad saw Mother at a party and fell in love her."

What was his reputation?

G.W.B.: "He was a star. He was a young man with a reputation for being considerate and polite but at the same time a person of tremendous abilities. I think Dad even today recollects the color of the dress and remembers Mother across the room at the party.

"It was one of those storybook meetings, and it has been a storybook marriage. They are in love. Forty-three years after their marriage, they are still in love.

"He has been quoted as saying when someone asked who he would like to be if he weren't George Bush that he would like to be Barbara Bush's other husband.

"We've had a good example of two people who have learned to live together and grow together. It's a fine example, not only for our little family but for the whole country."

Jeb Bush: "Barbara Bush is strong, loyal, and tough, but she is also very caring. She is one of the most organized persons you will ever meet. And she never gives up."

Give me the "lowdown" on the family. With five children, there must be a family clown. Who is the meanest, the fastest, the most brilliant? Who pinches their pennies?

Marvin: "George is a true family guy. He relishes the role of the older brother. He's protective of his younger siblings, and yet half the time he acts younger than all of us combined. He is ten years older than I am, but he's physically in great shape and a lot of fun.

"George tends to keep things loose at our family gatherings. I've heard stories that first kids are overachievers and very serious, but in our case we've got someone who, while achieving quite a bit, still keeps things light. He's fun to be around. He's a real character in the truest sense of the word. He'll keep everybody on their toes laughing."

Jeb: "George is the tightest with his money, that's for sure. He's always been careful. Marvin is the most personable and he has this great sense of humor. I'm the serious one."

Marvin: "Jeb is more serious-minded. He's quieter than the rest of us, and I think he's got great aspirations politically."

Yet he seems to be more of a public figure.

Marvin: "He is. It's kind of ironic. Jeb gets a lot of press, especially now that he is serving the State of Florida as Secretary of Commerce, but he is actually more private. His private life is important to him and his family.

"Neil is very outgoing. He's got a good sense of humor. He's probably as proud of his accomplishments as anybody because he had a serious dyslexic problem growing up and he's reached inside and worked really hard to overcome that.

"Like his older brother George, he is in the oil-and-gas business. He's got a technical background, which is useful because he's in the exploration side of the business. Neil has always had a bent toward science."

Jeb: "Neil is rather innocent, at least within the family context. He always thinks the best of someone. Yet he's been an excellent businessman, and not a pushover.

"Marvin is into financial management and investment counseling. He's given investment counsel to schools and foundations and endowments. Sometimes he may take on an individual's portfolio, but it would be for someone substantial.

"Doro, our sister, is probably a combination of everybody else's personalities. She can be shy or can sometimes take on Marvin's wry humor. She worked for a travel agency for a while. Now she has two children, so she's a full-time Mom, which is great."

Marvin: "When I think of Dorothy the word 'sensitivity' comes to mind. She is very thoughtful. She's always

The Vice President and his sons before appearing on NBC's "Today Show." (L-R) George W., Jeb, Marvin, and Neil.

Dave Valdez, The White House

The Bush family. (Top, L-R) Columba, Noelle, Jeb, Jebby, George P., Doro, Ellie, Bill LeBlond, Sam. (Bottom) Neil, Pierce, Sharon, Lauren, Marvin, Marshall, Margaret, Barbara, Jenna, the Vice President, George, Barbara, Laura.

thinking about how she can help somebody else. She's withdrawn and quiet.

"Of course, that's almost natural, since she grew up with four older brothers who were loud, boisterous, and athletic. She was probably overwhelmed. The fact that she survived is a major accomplishment.

"We all get along really well. We go through cycles where we talk to each other more at certain times than at other times. During a campaign we are particularly drawn together to help my parents. It's a great feeling."

Neil: "I agree. Jeb is the most serious. Marvin has the best sense of humor. George fits the 'big brother' syndrome. He does act younger than us all sometimes, just like Marvin said. He takes his role of older brother seriously, and it's great. Marvin said one word, 'sensitivity,' fits Dorothy. I'd say three words, 'love of family.' "

What have been the most painful family experiences?

Marvin: "When one of us has a problem, we share it with each other. We've been blessed, in one sense, in that all of us are happily married. So we haven't had to go through that kind of pain.

"I'm sure it was terrible for my parents and for my older siblings when my sister Robin passed away. That must have been an extraordinary thing to go through, for George particularly. I myself went through a lot of sickness, and people rallied around. There was that strength that comes from having love."

Barbara: [Speaking of Robin's death.] "It brought us much closer together. Many families are shattered by the same experience. Afterward George was unbelievable. He was so strong. He held me in his arms a lot and let me weep."

The dinner table. What was it like with so many personalities?

Marvin: "Conversations were never too heavy. We rarely talked about nuclear proliferation or how to balance the budget. We talked primarily about events that affected us, and what was going on in school or what was happening with our jobs or with our families. It was pretty low-key."

What about Christmas? Describe a Bush Christmas.

G.W.B.: "Christmas has been a time of joy, a time of anticipation, waiting for Santa Claus. There are songs and prayers, and sometimes family games.

"I can remember Christmases where less fortunate people were given gifts, and Dad made the point that we were celebrating God's gift. He always wanted us to know that Christmas was something other than just the receiving of gifts, that most importantly it had a spiritual significance and it was a time to be thoughtful to others."

Marvin: "Christmas was always great. When you grow up, some people really emphasize birthdays and that type of thing. My parents were very low-key about birthdays, but they felt that Christmas was a time when people shared their values and when everyone participated. It was an inclusive holiday.

"One thing I really love about Christmas at my parents' house is that you never know who is going to turn up. We would celebrate as a family the night before. We would go to late services at church and wake up the next morning to celebrate. Of course, my being the second-to-youngest, I couldn't wait to wake up to see if I'd gotten something good from Santa Claus.

"First we'd have breakfast together. It was a real lesson in patience for a young tot like me. Of course, the older kids would want to sleep in a little."

Was this in Houston or Washington?

Marvin: "In Houston. I always think of Christmas in Houston. Even after we moved to Washington, when my Dad became a Congressman, we would go back to Houston and go to St. Martin's Church, and it was a great feeling of continuity in a life where continuity was not always there. We were moving around some, and it was nice to have some of the same traditions.

"One year, sad but true, we were in a hotel. Still, just to have our family close together was important.

"After exchanging gifts we would have lunch, and typically we would have some guests. Sometimes it was someone who worked with my Dad or sometimes people would come by who didn't have a place to share Christmas and the spirit of the holidays. Sometimes it was someone who might be divorced or without a job. We would have this group of people around the table, and it was fun.

"Last year we had Mary Gall, who works with my Dad. She has adopted two little South American children who otherwise might not have had a big Christmas, with that big family experience. One of these kids was a little boy whose face was badly scarred. Years before he had been in a fire.

"And then I have a cousin named Mary Bush. She doesn't have a large family. Sometimes Lucy Cole comes over. Probably ten people come by. The Swedish Ambassador and his wife have come by for the last two or three years. They look forward to it and they bring one or two of their children if they happen to be around."

Where will Christmas be this year?

Marvin: "This year (1987) we will be at Camp David, which will be a novel experience. This is an important year for us. It's funny how it happened and it's typical of our family.

"For the past five or six years Margaret and I were the only children living in the Washington area. It was easy for us to come in for Christmas every year because we could drive up from Richmond, where Margaret's family lives, and come to Washington by midday for lunch. Usually Doro or one of my brothers would come each year. Since all of them were married, they each had obligations to their in-laws, who live in Texas, Florida, and Colorado.

"This year my sister Doro and Billy said they were going to come. Then George and Laura moved here to help with the campaign. Suddenly there were three of us. And then, about 3½ weeks ago, Neil called us and said, 'Marvin, do you think Mom and Dad would mind if we came for Christmas?'

"I replied, 'Mind? They'd love it.' He responded, 'I don't think there's room in the house.'

"I told him that either George or I would put him up or we'd find a place for him. 'Don't worry about that,' I said; 'that's the least concern—just come.'

"We knew this was going to be a pretty good Christmas, and we were all kind of scheming, because we knew that if four came, the likelihood was that the pressure would get to the fifth one and he would show up too.

"Finally Mom said, 'Look, we can't have a Christmas with four of our kids and not the fifth, so Jeb has to come.' I don't know what his plans were before, and I hope he didn't get into too much trouble at home, but he's coming now.

"Then my parents decided that it would be fun to go to Camp David, which is close by—about an hour away or maybe a little more. It's wonderful—we've all been there together one time before, for New Year's. There are different cabins for each of us, and we can meet together at Aspen Lodge. There is this gigantic living room with a great fireplace and a really warm feeling. We will probably all congregate there and yet be independent enough so that if any of our kids are misbehaving we could sneak them back out to the cabin. It's really going to be special. We'll be there for two days, which with a Presidential campaign is a lot of time. It's probably the equivalent of a week or so in any other year."

[Portions of these conversations took place following the Christmas holidays, 1987.]

Dorothy: "Camp David is really beautiful. It was wonderful. The fireplaces were going and the children had a great time. We watched a lot of videos together."

Neil: "It had been a while since we'd all been together at Christmas. We have a week each year in May, but Christmas all together is always something special. Camp David was perfect. Five kids, five in-laws, ten grandkids. Each family had its own lodge, so Mom didn't have to worry and work so hard. I videotaped Christmas morning. When we played it back later that day, my first reaction was that I was a horrendous cameraman. Then I realized I had truly captured the moment: utter chaos. It wasn't my camera work after all."

Jeb: "We always have a great time at these family gatherings. There was quite a contest at the bowling alley at Camp David this Christmas. I think Billy LeBlond, Doro's husband, did pretty well, and George P., my son, was great. I'll tell you who lost: George Bush, the Vice President. He did better in Iowa!

"And then Dad took George P. skeet-shooting at Camp David. One of the great pleasures for me is to see my children build a relationship with my parents. After about 15 minutes little George began to catch on and really learn. It was a great moment for both of them, and for me looking on. We'll never forget it."

Is there anything that's missing, anything that doesn't

*come through about the Vice President? Something about
his public image that doesn't square with the George Bush
you know?*

Jeb: "His complete sensitivity to people around him. He
is so personable. It's not a showy thing. I think about the
rehearsal dinners at our weddings. Marvin, perhaps, had
the biggest one. He had a great wedding in Virginia. My
rehearsal dinner was a small event with maybe ten people.
Dad would not get up and make a big speech or offer a
clever toast. But later he would sit down at his typewriter
and compose the most moving letter. It would express so
much."

Marvin: "There are a couple of things that don't come
through. One is his personal warmth. I've never understood why sometimes his public image is of someone a bit
colder or mechanical than he really is. I know him as a
loving, warm, thoughtful, sensitive man. I can talk to him
about anything at any time.

"Another thing is his sense of humor. He's a funny guy,
and I don't think that comes out in public.

"Whose fault is it? Who knows, maybe he's not the
media candidate, but I'm proud of that. To me that just says
he's not phony.

"The only other thing that doesn't always come across is
that my Dad is a doer. He's been a leader all his life. He's
made tough decisions. Most people expected him, or someone in his position, to just stay in New York, since that
would have been the easy thing to do. But what did he do?
He went to Midland, Texas, and at the time it was a new
horizon. When he accepted the job with the CIA, it was a
job that no one in his right mind would have accepted. It
was a tough job at a very tough time. And he had a choice:
He could accept it or not. Well, he did. So people who
suggest that he's not a strong and determined leader are
just mistaken."

Where were you during the time at the CIA?

Neil: "I was at Tulane when Dad was Director of the CIA. A group of us invited him down to the university. There were protestors and signs and yelling. None of it bothered me. Yes, it was my father they were protesting against, but I had a fundamental faith in his judgment and motives. I've never questioned anything he did.

"I felt the same during Watergate when he was Chairman of the Republican National Committee. I felt a relief for the party. I feel it now with him running for the Presidency. It is a sacrifice, but it's reassuring to me that a man of my father's caliber is willing to make such a sacrifice."

Marvin: "I was at the University of Virginia. So I was home a lot during that period. Charlottesville was just two hours from Washington.

"This was probably the only job that I've seen my Dad have in which I noticed the wear and tear."

Because he couldn't share?

Marvin: "That was a lot of it: He couldn't tell us what was going on. It's a tough job because not only did he have to perform the day-to-day tasks, the task at hand, but he also had to deal with an unbelievable public assault.

"Remember Frank Church's Senate confirmation hearings? They kept trying to politicize the issue. And my father kept saying, 'Let's focus on the issues at hand, what's going on in the agency. You're right—I'm a neophyte, but I'll go in and learn, I'll ask the types of questions you want.'

"We had to pretty much disavow any political intention for the next year-and-a-half. Actually, I don't think that was tough for him to do. He decided he was going to do the job, and like every other job he's accepted, he was going to do it right."

There are some who believe that, politically, he was leveraged into that position by rivals, precisely because they feared that Gerald Ford would make him his running mate.

Marvin: "Yes, that's interesting, though I never heard that twist until just recently myself. Who knows? Politics is a tough world. I wouldn't put it past anybody."

Barbara: "This was an interesting look at George's character. There are jobs which may seem to others beneath your dignity. But if you're learning it's not so important whether you're rewarded."

I've seen the Vice President in his work mode. His days go on forever. Everyone at the Bush Committee has caught "the spirit." Many work late into the night. And on the road he usually hits several states on the same day. When you're up at Kennebunkport and relaxing, what's a typical day? Does the Vice President play as hard as he works?

G.W.B.: "We usually start off with a family gathering in the morning and then Dad will go into another room to be briefed on the current day's events. As the Vice President, he has to keep up with what's happening in the world through a security intelligence briefing. That's a daily ritual. The rest of us eat a little breakfast.

"Some mornings will include fishing. George Bush loves to fish; he's an outdoorsman. He believes in enjoying the Creator's works. Typically, on the boat will be two or three family members. Sometimes we can sense Dad's moods, whether he wants to visit or just reflect and sit out there in the middle of the ocean. Most of us can sense that, and we just reflect with him as we enjoy the beauty of the water.

"There will usually be athletic activities in the afternoon, tennis or jogging. That takes up most of the day. In the evenings we all gather again around six o'clock. There may be fun board games or just visiting about the day's activities, dinner, and an early sack. It isn't hard to get everyone to bed early. The salt air really gets to you, and we've exercised so hard during the day that most of us are exhausted anyway."

Marvin: "I remember one afternoon up in Maine. My brother George and I were playing tennis when things got a little tight on the tennis court. I was about ten years younger than he was, and it got to an especially tense point in the match. I think I was fairly brash and was making sure he knew exactly what the score was. The next thing I knew he was chasing me up a fence.

"Sometimes it is a very competitive environment, in the sense that whatever you do, you are expected to do your best. At times when you're younger, you don't easily distinguish between healthy competition and trying to win. There is a difference.

"It's really a fun thing, the competition. Some of the funniest moments are when we get together as a family and exchange stories or information. We sometimes end up competing over that too."

G.W.B.: "Dad started jogging about ten years ago. It's a way for him to relax, get away and enjoy nature, and clear his mind. When he runs, he doesn't like to talk. He likes to concentrate on his running and also his thoughts.

"If one is a runner, and I'm a runner, you know that it's a great moment of solitude. Even though he might be surrounded by the Secret Service or other people, it's a chance for him to reflect on the day's coming events. Really, it's a very thought-provoking form of exercise. And he does it quite diligently, particularly on the campaign trail."

Every day?

G.W.B.: "Every day, as much as he can. In our family I'm the best runner, only because I'm the one most dedicated to it.

"When it comes to tennis, Marvin and Jeb are superb tennis players, and Neil too, for that matter. They are three very good athletes. I'm clearly the fourth, and I don't mind being that. I gave up a long time ago trying to whip my brothers in tennis. I just make a nice 'fill in' for them.

"By the way, on the tennis court, Dad holds his own with his kids, who are 30 years younger. He has very fast reflexes. He's also a competitor. He likes to win and he knows how to win. Yet he's a gracious winner. He's not someone to rub it in and make the other person feel bad. But we are all competitive, in the right sense of things, in a good spirit."

Your Mom loves books, and the Vice President does too. I've had conversations with them about their favorites. Did she get the boys reading or did that happen on their own?

G.W.B.: "I think it kind of happened on our own. I was never a great intellectual. I like books and pick them up and read them for the fun of it. I think all of us are basically in the same vein. We're not real serious, studious readers. We are readers for fun. C. S. Lewis has been a writer that Dad has read and enjoyed. And he reads the best-sellers. In recent years his reading time is overwhelmed by memos. They never end.

"Mother's love of reading relates to my brother, who was a serious dyslexic. He couldn't read and didn't know why. Finally Mother ferreted out the problem. Dyslexia, back in those days, was not well-known. She worked hard with Neil, disciplining, training, encouraging. She was the one who really spent the time making sure that Neil could learn to read the basics. As a result of this experience, Mother has decided to take the cause of illiteracy and dyslexia nationwide. She has made this a project of hers to help raise the flag of warning.

"Illiteracy is a problem that needs to be dealt with, and all of us need to pitch in and help. It's something that can be cured. As a nation, we need to bind together and unify to help our brothers and sisters learn to read."

It has economic implications as well.

G.W.B.: "The public service advertisements you see on television show a father trying to read to his kid. I love to read to my children. And Mother loves to read to her grandkids. The inability to read and express yourself to a child would be a very frustrating experience."

Does she do that? Does she read to her grandchildren?

G.W.B.: "Generally, one on one. In my case, as the father of twin daughters, two on one, because they both love to listen to the stories. My wife Laura is a librarian, so she also is very much into reading."

Tell me about your grandmother, Mrs. Prescott Bush. People say that she's had a great influence on the Vice President.

Jeb: "She's a pretty righteous lady. Her life's values are well set."

Marvin: "She's had a really strong influence on all of us—first on her children, and then kind of trickling down to our generation. She is one of the most spiritual people I have ever met, yet she's also very comfortable with people.

"When I say 'comfortable,' I mean she's never trying to impress anybody. I've never seen her try to improve her own situation at the cost of others. She's one of those very good and special people that you meet once in a lifetime.

"When you sit down and talk with my grandmother, you come away feeling better about yourself. There is a real gift to that. She's deeply devoted to her family. She's devoted to God.

"I think the saddest thing is that she still really misses her husband. I can sense it. That was 13 years ago, but even now, years later, she still thinks about him on a daily basis.

"It has been interesting for her to see her son running for President of the United States. When I'm with her, she says, 'Don't let them make your Dad travel so much.' She's a great Mom. In that sense she's a traditional Mom—a bit of a worrier for her son.

"She'll say, 'He looked a little tired the last time I saw him, and so, Marvin, your responsibility is to go back to the campaign and tell them to make him slow down.'

"Well, there's no way. If I went to the campaign with that story, they would tell me I was crazy. But they would all appreciate why she was doing that. She is truly a great lady."

What are the principles you taught your children?

Mrs. Prescott Bush (the Vice President's mother): "I taught them love. I taught them to love everybody, no matter what their background, and I taught them to be unselfish.

"One of my favorite verses in the Bible is First Corinthians chapter 13: 'Though I have the tongues of men and of angels and I have not love, I am nothing.' And, of course, the twenty-third Psalm.

"I taught my children to be kind and I taught them the golden rule: 'Do unto others as you would have them do unto you.' There are so many favorite Bible verses. They are all beautiful."

Faith played an important part in the family?

Mrs. Prescott Bush: "We prayed together as a family and read the Bible, and today I still do, every day. My husband and I used to read together in the morning and then again in evening. One of our favorite books was *A Diary of Private Prayers* by John Bailey. It has a devotional for every day and is a wonderful book. I still read it.

"There are many favorite books that have influenced me. H. Stewart Briscoe's *Getting into God* and John Stott's *Focused on Christ* are excellent.

"You never stop growing spiritually. Not too many years ago I visited L'Abri, Francis Schaeffer's retreat in Switzerland. Mrs. Schaeffer was there, and it was such a beautiful time to pray and talk about God, and learn about myself."

Did you ever have any instincts about young George, that he was destined for something important? Were there any clues or special characteristics that you noticed?

Mrs. Prescott Bush: "Well, I never heard him say he wanted to be President. The first time I heard that was in 1980, when he announced that he was going to run.

"The most consistent characteristic in his life, the characteristic I could see in him as a young child and that has stayed with him over the years, is his kindness to others. He was always worried about the other person. He wanted everyone to have a fair chance, and he was always looking out for the underdog. He has remained throughout all his life very considerate and very thoughtful."

Marvin: "China was a real eye-opener for my parents. Some people have asked my Dad, 'When did you first realize that you wanted to be President of the United States?' A great deal of his thinking about it occurred while he was in Peking. He looked around and saw people who had none of the basic freedoms that we had all taken for granted every day: waking up and starting your day realizing that you can do this or that. And not just with economic opportunities, but with political and religious freedoms. The Chinese people did not have the opportunity to express themselves. He really felt closer to the United States than at any other period in his entire career. When he came back, he felt so lucky to be an American."

Did the whole family visit China?

Marvin: "We did. The whole family, with the exception of my second-oldest brother, Jeb, who had just gotten married. Unfortunately, he couldn't join us. We all went over, and it was an eye-opener for me. I was 18 years old and curious by nature. It certainly helped inculcate a sense of patriotism. I had never really experienced anything but the United States. I had never been overseas.

"My parents met us at the airport. All I remember about landing is how dusty it was. There was no grass. Beauty was contrary to their general philosophy at that point, with anything beautiful to be looked down upon.

"There was a lot of dirt in Peking. It was a dirty city, and I ended up getting a cough as soon as I got there. In fact all of us did.

"The highlight of our trip was my sister's baptism. She was 16 but for some reason hadn't yet been baptized. But she was able to appreciate what was happening to her as much as anyone I ever knew, because she was older and realized the implications of it."

The Vice President: "As I understand it, she was the first person to be publicly baptized in China for over 40 years."

Marvin: "It took place in a nondenominational church in Peking. It was interesting because as you looked around you saw Black faces, Oriental faces, and white faces, but no Chinese. Everyone was from the diplomatic community, Ambassadors from other countries.

"Evidently the Chinese weren't allowed to go to church. They were singing songs like 'Onward Christian Soldiers,' and I don't think that was too consistent with Mao's belief.

"It was kind of neat, though. The church had an antiquated organ, and it wasn't the most beautiful church I've ever been in, but it was moving to see people who had to make an effort to seek the place out."

The Vice President: "There were only 20 or 30 people. And Dorothy was 16 years old—so beautiful."

Marvin: "My sister was the only one baptized. It was all very special. I was proud to be her stand-in as a godfather. It was so humble and yet so powerful to see this happening in the middle of the largest Marxist nation in the world. And, of course, it was nice to be by her side."

G.W.B.: "Every Sunday morning at Kennebunkport we all go to church together. Sometimes it's a huge crowd—all the children and grandchildren and the Secret Service. It is a little church by the sea. My sister was married there and I think my grandmother was married there. It's a tradition, a link to the past as well as to the future and to our faith."

Is that St. Anne's? I've heard the Vice President talk about it.

G.W.B.: "Yes, St. Anne's. The little kids pass the offering plate during the summer. I myself passed the offering plate, and now here I am, 41 years old, watching my own little girls passing the offering plate. There is this continuity of the generations that's so important in giving a person perspective. It's beautiful to see that in a living way."

The Vice President: "My favorite Bible passage? I'd

say the twenty-third Psalm. In my view that says it all.

"Favorite hymn? There are a lot of them, but without sounding militant, I love the Navy hymn. I get very emotional about those who serve in the military in this country.

"I think back to my three years of service and the young men who sacrificed their lives. And I think of those two FB-111 pilots lost in the raid on Qaddafi. I keep coming back to that Navy hymn, especially that third verse, 'God bless the men who fly . . .'

"And here I am with my family, lucky and blessed to be alive!"

- 8 -
Flowers for the Future

One sunny Sunday morning in July of 1987 I drove out to the Vice President's residence located on the grounds of the Naval Observatory. The Admiralty, as it was called, was a grand old Victorian home purchased by Nelson Rockefeller and given to the government as the permanent residence for the Vice President.

Somehow the Bushes had turned the place from a museum into a home. Maybe it seemed that way because they had lived there longer than any of the other Vice Presidential families. Or maybe it was because of that great and special warmth of the family. True to form, George "have-half" Bush was always unselfishly opening his doors to the children and their families and staffers.

One wonderful tradition was the Bush family Christmas party. It had grown so large that it spilled over onto consecutive evenings. These events were true celebrations and not just organized for political purposes. There was Barbara's giant Christmas tree, so colorful and so rich with tradition that it always ended up featured in full color in one of the women's magazines. The table was always filled with delicious food, and most of all, the rooms were packed with a wonderful variety of the nation's most colorful journalists, politicians, entertainers, and sports and business celebrities.

If the Bushes have wonderful memories in every corner of every room of their home, so do the rest of us. I'll never forget standing by that giant dining-room table, locked in a fascinating conversation about mutual friends in Poland with CIA Director William Casey, or a wonderful visit with television journalist Steve Bell, who had only recently come under the "Bush spell" and been adopted into the family. It was a delight to hear him recount his own experiences, confirming my impressions of that very special warmth and charm of the George Bush family.

The Vice President met me on the front porch as a cool summer breeze blew up from the wooded green park below us.

We sat in the library with coffee and cinnamon toast. From nearby bookshelves, autographed portraits of various world leaders looked on.

"I was a young man during the war, and I remember that there was almost an unspoken assumption that the victory would produce something like the nineteenth-century Concert of Europe, a generally peaceful world made up of basically compatible nations—in this case, of democracies rather than of monarchies.

"This was clearly Roosevelt's hope. We know now that Churchill had cautioned him about Soviet intentions. But Roosevelt dismissed Churchill's warnings by saying, 'I think that if I give [Stalin] everything I possibly can and ask nothing from him in return, he won't try to annex anything and will work with me for a world of democracy and peace.'

"Roosevelt died before he could fully see the futility of these hopes. Following Hitler's fall, Stalin reneged on the spirit, if not the letter, of his wartime agreements. The Yalta agreement in particular had called for democratic elections in liberated Europe. Instead, the areas under Soviet control experienced Stalin-imposed, Soviet-style regimes.

"Churchill insisted that the democracies must squarely face the full implications of Soviet actions. He gave those implications a name. 'From Stettin in the Baltic,' he said, 'to Trieste in the Adriatic, an Iron Curtain has descended across the continent.'

"It was not a commonly held view at the time. Yet it was a plea for realism, a plea for a clear strategy in approaching a new and unexpected world, a plea for courage to face reality rather than myth.

"Churchill suggested a strategy for keeping the Soviets from expanding the territory behind the Iron Curtain while at the same time keeping the peace.

"He called for help from the United Nations organizations, supported by the whole strength of the English-speaking world and all its connections. He said that peace required an extension of the relationship that had been primarily responsible for winning the war, at least on the Western front. At the time it was a great strategic vision.

"And of course he was right about the nature of the Soviet threat and about Soviet oppression. The Iron Curtain was not just an empty metaphor; it was and still is a real physical as well as moral presence.

"Three years ago on a trip to Germany, I visited a small German village called Moedelreuth. I'll never forget that town. Down the main street ran a high concrete wall topped with densely packed barbed wire. On our side the villagers were peacefully going about the ordinary business of their daily lives. On the Communist side, machine-gun-toting soldiers patrolled, and attack dogs ran on chains along the wall.

"Can anyone doubt what it means to live behind that wall? In the 30's and 40's too many people in the West looked to the Soviet Union with admiration. 'To travel from the capitalist world into Soviet territory,' said British writer John Strachey in those years, 'is to pass from death to birth.' This was not an uncommon view, particularly among intellectuals, even though Stalin was at the time murdering 30 million of his own people.

"Such views may have gotten a hearing then, but today we know the truth. We have the testimony of millions of pilgrims who have fled to the West—Solzhenitsyn, Scharansky, Sakharov, and so many others. Everyone today, even intellectuals, knows what it means to live behind the Iron Curtain."

It seems so obvious now; one wonders about the naivete. What errors are we making that will seem outrageous and naive to future generations?

"Churchill was very controversial. His 'Iron Curtain' speech was denounced by Eleanor Roosevelt. Clement Atlee gave it a cold shoulder. And there were others who disliked the speech. But by May 1946, polls showed that more than 80 percent of the American people favored a permanent Anglo-American military alliance.

"Churchill warned us not only of what the Soviets were presently doing but also of what they intended to do. He didn't believe that Soviet Russia desired war itself but rather that they desired the *fruits* of war and the indefinite expansion of their power and doctrine.

"And so it has been.

"Today there is no question about it: Churchill was right about what the Soviets were doing and about what they intended to do. His words almost immediately changed the way the Western world thought, and particularly the way Americans thought.

"In the end, of course, the alliance that emerged was broader than the one that Churchill envisioned.

"Today NATO includes as members or close associates not only Britain, Canada, and the United States, but most of the democracies of Europe."

You mentioned the United Nations. I never thought of Churchill as a great booster.

"Oh, yes, absolutely. Of course he would be horrified

with the results today. While he was right about the character of the threat and right in his strategic vision of an alliance of democracies, in another sense his worldview proved both faulty and narrow.

"It was faulty in the sense that the United Nations, in which he had placed such hope, proved by and large a great disappointment. Yes, the U.N. had some successes, but they were mainly in the economic and social areas. For example, the World Health Organizations did outstanding work, and the U.N. High Commission on Refugees, despite inefficiency and infighting, saved the lives of millions of people.

"Nevertheless, in the crucial area of peacekeeping, the U.N. fell far short of the world's hopes for it. It showed little ability to prevent wars. And once wars had started, it showed little ability to stop them.

"The current war between Iran and Iraq, for example, has taken hundreds of thousands of lives and has presented the world with a major escalation in the use of chemical weapons. It is just one example of the impotence of the U.N. as a peacekeeper."

You were once the United Nations Ambassador. Did you come away with any conclusions about why the U N. hasn't worked?

"There is a fundamental problem with an organization whose charter gives a nation of half a million people the same single vote in the General Assembly that it gives China, with 1.2 billion people. It is true that resolutions of the General Assembly are not binding in international law, but it is also true that the often-outrageous and irrelevant resolutions passed by the General Assembly diminish the U.N.'s overall standing in the court of world opinion.

"The U.N. is useful for international discussion, but too often in the last decades it has become a forum for those who disdain democratic values and who seek to undermine them. It has sometimes become a forum for the practitioners of terror and violence and for their propaganda. "Having served in the U.N. and having watched it quite carefully during the last 15 years, I can tell you that the increase in bloc voting is very damaging. I lament the propagandistic attacks on the U.S., I lament the one-sided and incessant attacks on the State of Israel. And though I do not fault the Secretary General himself, it is clear that the U.N.'s role as a peacemaker and peacekeeper is minor at best."

You said that Churchill's view of the world was too narrow, and yet with the exception of his idealism about the United Nations, he was almost prescient throughout his life.

"Churchill's strategic view was almost exclusively European-centered. He referred to the British Empire, but as an extension of Britain itself, not as separate territories with independent strategic identities.

"At the Yalta Conference he made the claim, 'While there is life in my body, no transfer of British sovereignty [over the colonies] will be permitted.'

"Yet despite his opposition, by the time he died nearly all the Empire was gone. Independent nations stood in its place, and in the place of all the empires of Europe.

"Colonization has not meant that Europe has become unimportant. Europe remains today the focus of security and strategy for the United States, for Europe remains today the free world's king on the global chessboard. It may not be the most powerful piece on the board, but if the other side can strip it of its defenses and trap it, the game is as good as over.

"Nevertheless, the chessboard and the game itself are larger and more complex than Churchill foresaw.

"Churchill anticipated and sought to prevent a major, all-out war between the West and the Soviet Union. And the NATO alliance has achieved his goal. The United States, Europe, and the Soviet Union have been at peace for 42 years now. For Europe this is by far the longest peace in this century.

"Major war has been prevented, but smaller conflicts have not. There have been more than 140 little wars since World War II. Together they have claimed up to ten million lives. Almost all of these wars have been in regions that were once under European colonial rule, either in Asia, Africa, or the Americas. Many of these conflicts have been vehicles for the expansion of Soviet power and influence. This was particularly true in Korea and Vietnam."

There was criticism in the 1960's that America had its own imperialistic or colonial aims. The French abandoned Vietnam and we stepped in.

"That's entirely false.

"The Prime Minister of Singapore, Lee Kuan Yew, recently addressed a joint session of Congress. I have great respect for him. I admire the keenness of his insight. In his world vision, Prime Minister Lee is in some respects a modern Churchill.

"To Congress that day he described East Asian societies as 'on the move.' He said they were 'seething with restless energy, transforming their ancient civilizations into modern industrial societies.'

"Prime Minister Lee told me that he credits East Asia's success in part to American actions over the past four decades, actions that included the Korean and Vietnamese wars.

"By holding the Korean Communists north of the 38th parallel, the United States insured not only that South Korea would remain free, but that Japan would remain tied to the West and would continue to develop as a nonmilitary, commercially oriented democracy. Japan has become the economic engine of free Asia.

"By taking a stand in Vietnam, the United States gave Thailand, Malaysia, and Indonesia time to rally their people against Communist insurgencies in their own countries and, together with Singapore, to develop more stable political systems and vibrant economies.

"Without the courage and commitment of America, none of this would have been possible. Without the courage and commitment of America, all of East Asia might today be sunk in a Communist swamp, a swamp as stagnant and oppressive as that in which so many millions of Vietnamese and Cambodians have perished since we left Southeast Asia more than a decade ago. A swamp from which more than a million others have fled, by boat and over land, by any means they could, to find their way to the promised land, to find their way to America.

"If America was imperialistic, she should never have let go of Japan and the Philippines, and on and on the list goes."

Does democracy in the Philippines represent a trend?

"I'm convinced of it. The people in the Pacific Basin revere democracy. We used to hear it said of so many developing, newly industrialized countries that they were not ready for democracy. Well, the Filipino people showed not only that they were ready but that they wouldn't wait.

"The Philippines have had key elements of a democratic system off and on for decades. Eventually the Philippine people wanted a true democracy, a strengthened and perfected democracy. In their yearning, there were millions on the Asian mainland, and many of them put their lives on the line for the privileges that we Americans take for granted.

"Now, as a result, the truly democratically elected government in Manila is a beacon of hope for all who seek to build democracy around the world.

"Five years ago there was only one democratically elected government in Central America, and that was Costa Rica. Today there are democratically elected governments not only there but in Honduras, El Salvador, Guatemala, and the newly independent Belize as well.

"In Central America, only Nicaragua suspends all civil rights, including freedom of speech and freedom of the press. In Central America, only Nicaragua suppresses all opposition political parties. Only Nicaragua refuses to enter into dialogue with its political opponents. Among current Central American governments, only Nicaragua orders the execution of political dissenters. Only Nicaragua has harassed not only the Catholic Church (and humiliated the Pope when he visited Managua), but has persecuted Pentecostals, Mormons, and Jews. Only Nicaragua receives support from terrorist states and terrorist organizations all over the world. Only Nicaragua provides arms to Communist terrorists in democracies like Colombia, El Salvador, and Costa Rica.

"Only Nicaragua swims against the democratic tide."

Mr. Vice President, some say that the conflict in Nicaragua hurts us so badly in public relations that we would be much better off to let it drop. Whatever our intentions, America is sometimes viewed by the world as interventionist.

"There are strategic concerns as well. Churchill's vision of a transatlantic alliance to guarantee Europe's peace was based on several assumptions about the world order. Perhaps the most important was that the United States would not be preoccupied with challenges on its own borders. That was a good assumption. It had been true for most of

American history. And because it was true, America was able to go to the defense of European democracies twice in Churchill's lifetime.

"If Soviet- and Nicaraguan-sponsored insurgencies should spread throughout Central America, this premise would cease to be true. And the world would then have to ask the question: Is America still able to help defend Europe, that free-world king on the global chessboard? And if not, will Europe have to cut a deal with the Soviets? And if Europe does, will the Pacific Rim countries have to follow?

"This is what I meant earlier when I said that today's global chessboard is larger and more complex than in Churchill's time.

"Still, he was very right about one thing. Churchill believed that the judicious use of strength when threats were small was the best guarantee that threats would not become big. Of course, his cries of warning during Hitler's rise were ignored.

"Today, with a relatively small amount of aid to the freedom fighters, we can stop the threat to the region from the Sandinistas and support the people struggling for freedom and democracy in Nicaragua. We're talking about *aid*. Not American troops and not direct American involvement—just *aid*. A democratic Nicaragua is indispensable to a peaceful, stable, democratic Central America. That's why giving aid to the freedom fighters is like taking out an insurance policy for freedom and democracy all over the region."

The liberation theologians would be contemptuous of your chessboard analogy. They would say that the hungry and poor of Central America are only seeking a way out of their poverty cycle, and are too weak to represent a threat in the world balance of power.

"Of course it is Soviet military advisors and tanks and helicopters in Central America that threaten to tip the balance, and not the poor people who we more than anyone want to help. But shouldn't people who want to escape poverty fight *against* Communism and not for it?

"Look at the two sides of the Iron Curtain—Eastern Europe and Western Europe. Which is poor and which is not?

"Look at Southeast Asia—Vietnam, Cambodia, and Laos—on the one hand, and at Thailand, Malaysia, Indonesia, and Singapore on the other. Where do more people live in poverty? Where is there prosperity and opportunity?

"Look at our own hemisphere. In Cuba, Castro turned a thriving economy into a basket case. Nicaragua has slipped steadily downhill. Compare these countries to Brazil, Argentina, Colombia, or Costa Rica.

"Or look at the Soviet Union itself, a country where ordinary people must wait in line for almost everything (although it's different if you're in the ruling class), a country that has found a way to make some of the most fertile land in the world disastrously unproductive. They blame the weather, and maybe they're partly right, although countries that border on the Soviet Union don't have the same problems.

"Today in Africa and India and all over the world, those who once flirted with the Soviet model are turning their eyes to the West. They have found, as people everywhere have found, that the answer to poverty is not Communism, not slavery, not dictatorial socialism, but *freedom*.

"It was Trotsky who said, 'The dictatorship of the Communist Party is maintained by recourse to every form of violence.' And he was right: It must be so, because free men and women will fight to remain free. And those in chains will struggle to break their chains, as we've seen these last 40 years in East Germany and Hungary, in Czechoslovakia and Poland.

"The challenge before us today is to help those who, in smaller conflicts, defend freedom and champion democracy, demonstrating the courage for what John Kennedy called the 'long twilight struggle.'

"The challenge before us today is to face with courage, unity, and resolve all attacks on free societies and free institutions."

What was your relationship with President Eisenhower?

"I never met with him privately. I did go up to the Eisenhower farm with members of Congress. He had great respect for my father. They were close."

What would be your assessment of the Eisenhower Presidency?

"Stability, respect for the office of the Presidency. He was not flamboyant, but he was coming off the war as a genuine hero. He brought a certain decency and honor to the White House. I think there was a tendency on the part of some of the more liberal press to attack him as not being 'fully engaged.' But he rose above all that.

"Actually, he was President during a time when the country was enjoying pretty good prosperity. The Eisenhower Presidency wasn't marked by flamboyance and erratic stops and starts, but rather by a stability which had its underpinning in decency and honor."

What about the management style of the last two Presidents? Reagan and Carter seem to represent opposite extremes. And how do the two styles compare with your own?

"Jimmy Carter, whether fairly or not, got credit for knowing everybody who played on the White House tennis court. And President Reagan has been a master delegator. He has a feel for very good people, and then he delegates responsibility to them.

"I think I would be somewhere in between. When I ran my oil business I delegated, but I would also be intimately familiar with what the top people were doing. I think this is good for the morale of people and I also think it's good management.

"I've tried to do that in every job I've had. At the CIA I made my imprint by moving people around, getting good people involved, and then staying in touch with them every single day.

"When Jimmy Carter came in, he treated the CIA almost as if there were some corruption there and he was going to ferret out all the people that were violating the law. Well, the agency is much better than that. The staff is manned by decent people. And so although I did make changes when I was there, I depended on career people and stood up for them. They knew I was a leader who wasn't afraid to defend them before the Congress or to the media.

"I think you have to be out in front of your troops in a war, in combat, or in management. It was true when I was running a business. Some of the nicest things that are said about my days in business come from people who were in the field themselves, the tool-pushers, the drilling superintendents, the roughnecks—and that pleases me very much.

"Each person needs to have his own management style. That's the way I've done it, and I think it is a very good approach. We still have career people at the United States Mission to the United Nations who comment favorably on my time there. They knew I followed their work and I cared about them. I think there is something to that: a broad management sense, but personable."

Any thoughts on the strengths and weaknesses of the Kennedy Presidency?

"Kennedy had flamboyance and style. His youth and wit captured the imagination of the people. He was living in a different era in terms of how the press treats public figures, and I expect that if he had been living in this time he might have been treated a bit more harshly.

"In a sense I'm glad that didn't happen, because I have enough respect for the Presidency that I don't like to see it diminished in any way. Many aspects of Kennedy's personal life would be more seriously examined and condemned today; there is no question about that. But having said that, I don't want to cast any stones on his memory because it was a different time.

"If you're asking for a political evaluation or an evaluation of the substance of his administration, I would have to say that the reality doesn't equal the myth.

"People forget that Kennedy was in fairly serious political trouble before he was assassinated, in terms of domestic legislation, and it took Lyndon Johnson to fulfill the Kennedy agenda. Many things that Kennedy wanted to do were done by Lyndon in the name of the fallen martyr. So I think an objective assessment of Kennedy's accomplishments coupled with the new age of personal accountability that we are living in leaves the jury still out on the Kennedy Presidency."

And Johnson?

"I knew Johnson quite well. He was a very complicated fellow—a consummate politician of the old-school, old-style type. Again, he was living in a different age. Here was a Senator who accumulated his family wealth while in the Senate through the licensing of television stations. That was acceptable in those days; nobody thought anything about it. Today you wouldn't be able to do that.

"Still, I give Johnson credit for a certain perseverance. I disagreed with a lot of the programs that he enacted, because now I think the young people in this country are having to pay the piper. We warned that the programs would be extraordinarily expensive and would be a burden on a lot of people who wouldn't participate. But he got things done because he was a strong leader.

"His demise was the Vietnam War. Yet as I look at Vietnam today and see it brutalizing its neighbors, as I see the massacres in Cambodia, pressing and crushing the spirit of the people, I think we ought to remove the onus of an immoral war from the memory of Lyndon Johnson. Our kids were taught that he was wrong, and that if we got out there would be some form of democracy. Well, there isn't. The last vestiges of democracy died when the last U.S. soldier left South Vietnam.

"My conclusions about Vietnam are different from those of the liberals; our purpose wasn't immoral. But the experience did reaffirm the Douglas MacArthur dictum: Don't get involved in a land war in Asia, and don't get involved in a war without the support of the people. You can't win."

Gerald Ford?

"Decency; a very uncomplicated, straight-shooting individual. I probably know him better than the others. I can tell you that I have great respect for him. He has a good family, and he has held it together. They've been through quite a bit, particularly with Mrs. Ford's illness. He stood right by her, holding her hand and backing her. I respect that kind of love for family.

"Since he came into office without having been elected, and then being there only a short time, I think it's hard to reach conclusions on his accomplishments. But I think the major thing he did was to lift up the nation when it was distraught after the Watergate days."

With President Reagan, were there any private realities that were contrary to the public perceptions?

"Because of President Reagan's management style, he got accused of being detached. But I see him every single day, and he is not detached. He is very much interested in the key, large-picture issues. He is less interested than some would be in all the detail, but he is not detached.

"The side I see that others don't is the kindness and the sense of humor. He is always willing to see something good in a person, even those who attack him. I think there is something very decent and honorable about that. The rest of it is pretty well written publicly. He's been unfailingly kind to Barbara and me, and that has made being Vice President pretty easy."

During President Reagan's first year Edwin Meese was being called the "assistant President." The implication was that he and not President Reagan was the secret to success. And then he left that inner circle. For a while Michael Deaver was referred to as a master of public relations, and the story was that the Reagan success was style over substance, that it was all Michael Deaver's magic. And then he left that inner circle, and for a while James Baker was lauded as the one with great executive capabilities and the secret to Reagan's success. Yet each of these men saw their policies, or in some cases their integrity, diminished when they left that circle. Is there a case to be made that they looked good because they were close to Reagan instead of the other way around? That he may have had more of the talent than he has been given credit for?

"I think each of those people would tell you that the President made more of the decisions than the press gave him credit for. But each of them in varying degrees made a significant contribution. There is no doubt that Reagan was the guiding strength behind the policies.

"His strength came from a handful of principles that he believed in and stayed with. There could be variety, there could be compromise, there could be give-and-take, but those basic principles were his guidelines. He was able to project them throughout the entire administration. He preached less government, less taxes, and a consistent position on the social issues. I think this philosophy permeated his inner circle, so that the people went out and managed things for him according to those principles."

We've talked about Mikhail Gorbachev. Any contradictions there?

"He's very charming. He came in the very first day he was in office with that affability and sense of humor. He makes everyone feel relaxed. But when I first talked to him about human rights, he flared up. You could see the anger and steel.

"I was talking about the need for the Soviets to adhere to the Helsinki Accord and have more respect for human rights. But he flared up and reacted with a very uninformed response about our own civil rights problem. Was he grandstanding or was he really that much out of touch? It was almost like young kids fighting and saying, 'My old man is tougher than yours.'"

What about Pope John Paul II?

"Kind and well-informed. Meeting alone with him, I could just sense that I was in the presence of a person deeply committed to peace, deeply committed to the betterment of mankind.

"He has said, 'Freedom develops best if it keeps to the rules of morality.' It is a great lesson that this nation once carefully followed and must follow again. He is right; we must teach our children the difference between right and wrong, honesty and dishonesty, liberty and license. And we must teach it in our schools as well as our churches and homes.

"He is a very bright man. We weren't into our discussion very far before I realized that this is a man who not only possesses a great native intelligence but is also very well-informed about what is happening in the world. Most impressive."

Francois Mitterand?

"I was the first American official to have contact with Mitterand. There was a bit of concern when we learned that he was bringing Communists into his cabinet. What would the impact be for the defense of Western Europe? Others worried about the economic fallout for France with his rapid move to the left in pursuit of the socialist model.

"Actually, he's quite subdued and laid-back, but in the matters of East and West he's been very strong. One of the great speeches of this generation was delivered by Mitterand at a time of great turmoil in Europe. The debate was on in Germany and across Western Europe: Should the Pershing missiles be deployed? He laid out the importance of the alliance coming together and the importance of a realistic look at the Soviet Union. There was an intellectual integrity in his logic and in his world overview that only a true statesman could have. I have great respect for him."

Margaret Thatcher?

"I know her well and respect her. She is very open and very easy to converse with. Also, she is very loyal to the special friendship between the United States and the United Kingdom.

"On a recent visit here she was baited by liberal journalists. They were trying to get her to denounce the President by saying that the Iran controversy had diminished him. She stood up and took them on and did it with great strength and character. She made very clear the reality of the world—namely, that the United States is indeed the respected leader of the free world. Those performances with four networks and Face The Nation, all in the period of 24 hours, were sterling. They were vintage Thatcher.

"The American people saw not only her own strength but also her loyalty to that special relationship between the United Kingdom and the United States of America, and her proper recognition that the United States and its President represent the leader of the free world. There is no doubt about it—she is one of the great leaders of this generation and one of Britain's most effective Prime Ministers."

Helmut Kohl?

"One of the advantages of being Vice President is that you get to know these leaders on a very personal basis. I've been with Chancellor Kohl many times, and he is a strong leader, very straightforward.

"He survived elections that threatened to take Germany into a much more liberal posture. He did it by standing up strongly for what he believes. As a true statesman he put the interests of his country and the interests of freedom above his own political career. He risked being misunderstood as he fought off the radical excesses of the so-called peace movement led by the Greens. And he won when the people of Germany stood with him and determined that they would not give in to Soviet blackmail.

"He's been a good and loyal friend of the United States, and vice versa. He is a leader who is well-respected. He's had difficulties, but he seems to have remained strong."

One night, after an exhausting day of appearances in different states, the Vice President invited me to the front cabin aboard Air Force Two. He was tired but relaxed, his work for the day behind him now. In a few hours he would be landing at Andrews Air Force Base and then would helicopter across Washington D.C. to his residence at the Admiralty.

With the sparkling lights of American cities drifting slowly by in the darkness below us, I talked to the Vice President about his fears and hopes for the world.

What could go wrong? After years of top-secret intelligence briefings, did he have any nightmares? What were the dangers?

"Sure, I have concerns.

"I see the mounting world debt and I see our own economic challenges. There is still a terrible famine in Africa. There is a war in the Middle East that, like a meat grinder, is chewing up thousands of Iranian and Iraqi young men. There is the injustice of apartheid. We haven't solved the problem of drug addiction. We haven't found a cure for cancer.

"But all of this doesn't mean that we haven't made progress. The world has always been a dangerous place, but it is also a place filled with hope, and decency, and honor."

The statistics on drug use in this country are alarming. In addition to our trade deficit, more than a hundred billion dollars flows out of this country to purchase illicit drugs. The money then comes back, untaxed, to compete with legitimate dollars for investments in real estate and property. Of course, the social dimensions are staggering. Every family seems to be eventually touched by the problem.

"It's a great tragedy, and it will not be easily solved. Yet we have made a dent in it. Cocaine use is down. Even marijuana use is down among high-schoolers. We are the first administration that has made an all-out effort on both the supply side (by trying to interdict narcotics coming into the country) and the demand side (through education and public relations).

"Nancy Reagan has been effective. She has gone to the private sector and also to the schools to warn the young people in this country against the use of narcotics."

From time to time we see news reports of giant "drug busts" in which tons of heroin or cocaine are confiscated. Still, the availability of these drugs seems unaffected. How is our interdiction program working?

"First, we have changed the laws so that we can use military assets to help civilian agencies like the DEA, the FBI, and Customs to interdict narcotics.

"Second, we have formed the National Narcotics Border Interdiction System. This is a nationally coordinated drug-interdiction program of which I am chairman. We have interdicted huge amounts of drugs, although we still have a large job ahead of us.

"In this day of sparse budget resources, we have increased the antinarcotic funding by 200 million dollars, and this amount would have been more if we had had our way. So some good things are happening. Three years ago, 40 percent of the population of Miami wanted to leave the city because of crime and narcotics. Now the morale has totally turned around. There is still a narcotics problem in Miami, but we've made progress, having done more than any other administration on this issue.

"On the demand side our administration, with Mrs. Reagan in the lead, is focused on helping educational programs in the schools and in the communities and on encouraging the private sector to teach people that the use of narcotics is deadly.

"This is a number-one issue on the polls. When you ask 'What most concerns you?' drugs in school is always near the top of the list. And our administration is really going after this problem. You no longer hear talk about the legalization of marijuana or of narcotics, and under our administration you never will. I am strongly opposed to legalization, and we've got to keep pushing away on the demand side."

What about Colombia, Mexico, and Panama?

"We're getting much better cooperation from some of these countries. We've had some problems on the border that are still there, but there has been much better cooperation from Peru. The Jamaicans have been magnificent.

"Looking back over these past years that I've served as Vice President, international cooperation is much better, but it's still a major problem.

"The good thing for our neighbors to the south is that they now realize that it's their problem as well as ours. Previously they thought they might get some money out of the narcotics traffic, since some of their farmers were profiting. Now they realize that it is destroying their own children and their own societies. For the first time, over the last couple of years, some of these countries are giving us significant help.

"There still are some corrupt officials in various countries. We have some in our own system, but what we've got to do is find them and put them in jail, thereby breaking the back of narcotics use and narcotics supply in this country."

Where does our criminal justice system break down? Is it at the police level, the prisons, the courts?

"I think it breaks down in several areas. There are judges who are permissive, who seem to be more interested in the criminals than in the victims of crime. We have tried to correct this problem through federal appointments, by people who will interpret the Constitution and not try to legislate from the bench.

"Then there is the problem of overpopulation in our prisons. I've talked with those intimately involved in trying to bring the narcotics traffickers to justice in Dade County, Florida. The case load is unprecedented, and the U.S. Attorney's office there is simply undermanned. As we struggle for additional support for him, we run up against some very serious budget constraints, including Gramm-Rudman (which we support), which in some areas does cause strain.

"So the problem is a combination of permissiveness and undermanned facilities, prisons, and courts, and we are struggling to reorder our priorities to see that we can help in all these areas."

Where do you stand on capital punishment?

"Unfortunately, there are instances in our society of exceptionally terrible crimes, and there must be a credible penalty on the federal books to respond to these cases. I strongly support capital punishment for crimes involving murder, treason, or espionage. The American people overwhelmingly realize that judges sometimes have to impose the death penalty in certain clearly defined and particularly heinous crimes.

"I also support increased jail sentences for certain criminals, particularly repeat offenders."

There was a charge in the media that Jerry Falwell has influenced the administration in its appointment of federal judges. And yet Richard Hammer, an evangelical attorney, says that he has found only four out of 748 federal judges that are evangelical Christians, who represent 40 percent of the population. The charge on the one hand is that evangelicals are taking over the judicial process and on the other hand that they are excluded.

"I don't know of any recommendation to any position made by Jerry Falwell. But that last criticism troubles me greatly.

"I don't think anybody should be excluded. What the President tries to do is to pick those judges that are best qualified. I can assure you that there is no deliberate exclusion of people because of their faith.

"My view has been, and I've taken a few shots for it, that it is time for all people to participate. I believe in separation of church and state, but I also believe in participation in politics. The legislative, the executive, and the judicial branches should reflect America's tolerance and plurality.

"I hope this gentleman is not asserting that there is a deliberate policy to keep worthy, legal talent from serving on the bench, because we don't want it to be that way."

Was the Senate's rejection of Robert Bork a mistake?

"I'm convinced that Justice Kennedy will serve the nation well, but I think the rejection of Robert Bork was very political and unfair.

"I have known Bob Bork for 20 years, and he is a brilliant jurist and scholar of the Constitution who would have had respect for judicial precedent. But when the President sent his name to Capitol Hill, Senator Kennedy greeted him like a pit bull meeting the mailman.

"They distorted Bork's positions. Mary Ann Glendon, a professor at Harvard Law School, examined the record. She concluded, and I quote, 'Judge Bork is likely to be a strong supporter of women's rights.'

"And why is that? Because the most important legal gains that American women have made in the twentieth century have been through legislation, and Judge Bork believes the Court should interpret the laws, not make them.

"I believe the American people want a court that will balance the rights of victims with the rights of criminals, a court that will not attempt to rewrite the Constitution just as we celebrate its 200th birthday."

Let's talk about poverty. Some say there is a crime-poverty cycle. Where are we headed with entitlements? We now have families who are apparently trapped, with three generations on welfare. Are we going to end up like some of the European nations in which the productivity of a few subsidizes the many?

"I refuse to surrender the high ground on compassion for the disadvantaged to those whose only answer is a giveaway. My emphasis is on education. The surest way to win the war against poverty is to win the battle against ignorance.

"Generation after generation of immigrants have come to our shores, desperate and destitute, and yet have extricated themselves from poverty and become a part of mainstream American life. How did they do it? Not by the actions of government. They did it with strong families, an emphasis on education, and hard work. Those values have worked in the past, and they will work today.

"How do you pass on a sense of work as rewarding and important to someone who has never experienced it? One way is to require work, with appropriate exceptions, in exchange for welfare.

"This is not a punitive measure, designed to penalize those who seek government assistance. It is a measure to increase the self-image of those who may never have worked, to help them find the connection between the effort they make and the reward they get. What is hard is most valued.

"Another way is to turn over the management or even the ownership of public housing to responsible tenant groups. When this was tried in St. Louis, it resulted in improved housing and gave the tenants a sense that they were taking charge of their lives.

"Beyond that, homesteading preference could be given to stable, two-parent families with a working head of household that remain in disadvantaged areas, who offer a role model other than the pimp and the pusher for the youngsters of their neighborhood."

South Africa is one of those crises that won't go away. One source suggests that we import 80 percent of our strategic minerals from Russia and South Africa. We need those South African resources to defend the West, and yet we are morally weakened by appearing reluctant on the issue of apartheid.

"The Republic of South Africa is by far the richest, most powerful, and most highly developed country in the sub-Sahara. It is the most influential country in Southern Africa, a superpower in the region. And of course its reserves of minerals are vitally important to the West. So is its location at the tip of the continent.

"But South Africa is really a pariah state. The vastly outnumbered Afrikaners, acting out of fear, have constructed a racist system of apartheid to ensure their political and economic supremacy. That system is morally repugnant to all who believe in human liberty, and we can't rest until it is ended.

"We've got to balance our strategic interests in a stable, pro-Western South Africa with the equally pressing political and moral imperative to change South Africa's social system. We have to appreciate that the long-range political interests of the United States will only be served by the elimination of apartheid.

"We need to convince all South Africans, black and white, that the United States seriously desires the end of apartheid. We have taken positive, effective, and tangible steps to achieve this goal. The passage of the 1986 Comprehensive Anti-Apartheid Act puts in place strong sanctions against South Africa and sets conditions for their removal. Unfortunately, the political and economic effects of the sanctions have been marginal to negative. We believe that the South African government has made little progress in dismantling apartheid and that Black South Africans have been set back economically.

"In addition, we have worked closely with the business community to encourage adherence to the Sullivan principles of fair employment practices. These practical programs which build and strengthen the Black South African community politically and economically are the key to peaceful power-sharing there.

"The 1986 Comprehensive Anti-Apartheid Act is the law of the land, and we have faithfully implemented that law. The debate over sanctions was about means, not ends. But sanctions are not a policy in and of themselves. Under the present circumstances I would not recommend further sanctions. Rather, we must continue to use diplomacy and negotiations for constructive change.

"Some people think that this will achieve nothing, but it's not true. I believe that our policy in the past seven years has made some small progress, and fresh initiatives should acknowledge new realities and focus clearly on the central issue of political change in South Africa. We should encourage the development of strong and democratic Black political institutions to aid in the peaceful transition to majority rule. American trade unions, religious groups, and other groups should work with their South African counterparts to help develop such democratic institutions. This has already begun to happen, and it will really be the key."

Is the nuclear nightmare diminished with INF? There has been talk about a thaw in the cold war.

"If there is one thing I've learned in my years of dealing with Soviet leaders, it is that anyone who tells you that he or she knows for sure what's going on there is a fool.

"We all know, but sometimes fail to remind ourselves, that the Soviet Union is a closed society, with power based on secrets and systematic manipulation of information, even to the point of outright deception. We were reminded of this when we learned about the lengths to which the Soviets have gone to compromise the security of the U.S. Embassy in Moscow.

"Some sophisticated types say that Americans are naive to be shocked about this sort of thing. But we are not the only people who react this way. Once, when I was meeting with President Zia of Pakistan in Moscow in a room we knew was bugged, he burst out, 'Thank God I do not have to live and work in a country like this!' Another time, at a Moscow meeting with Prime Minister Suzuki of Japan, one of the senior Japanese officials present said loudly to the walls, 'I hope the Russians heard every word we said. They won't like any of it.'

"So we do not know the Soviets in the way we can know other countries. Perhaps someday we will know more. For now we have to deal with the Soviet Union as it is, not as we may wish it to be."

Yet we've talked about Gorbachev. Perhaps there is a chance for some stability at the top.

"I've been to Moscow three times as new leaders were installed. I don't expect to be going again soon for that purpose. Mr. Gorbachev is a strong and vigorous leader who might well lead the Soviet Union into the twenty-first century. In our dealings with the Soviets, we should take that into consideration.

"In the past, America has had trouble learning how to deal consistently with this secretive, enigmatic society. I remember that when Jimmy Carter took office in 1977, he decided to abandon the arms-control positions that President Ford had developed after his meeting with Brezhnev in Vladivostok. President Carter wanted to try for deeper cuts. He presented his own position to the Soviets, and it took them by surprise.

"The Soviets reacted by rejecting the Carter proposals out of hand. And Jimmy Carter, instead of sticking to his guns, went right back to some of the earlier positions. He lost any chance he had to draw the Soviets into serious negotiations.

"This kind of behavior gets us nowhere. It gets us nowhere to squeal in delight every time the Soviets give us a conciliatory signal. It gets us nowhere to react irrationally when they do something outrageous and say that we won't deal with the Soviets under any circumstances. When a real crisis comes, a Korean Airlines plane shot down or a Nick Daniloff in jail, there have to be open lines of communication. And we must respond resolutely.

"Both kinds of overreaction ignore the central truth of U.S.-Soviet relations. After dealing with the Soviets through the reigns of four different leaders, I know that we cannot formulate U.S. policy by trying to figure out what is on their minds at any given moment. Much of the time we are not going to know just who the Soviets really are."

There has been criticism that this administration's foreign policy failed to pursue linkage in our relationship with the Soviets.

"These past years I have been part of a U.S. effort to become tougher and steadier in our dealings with the Soviets. We have developed a four-part agenda that we consistently refer to, so that the different U.S. interests will not have center stage one day only to be forgotten the next day.

"The Soviets would prefer to talk to us about nothing except arms control. But we have stood our ground, and over time we have seen them become willing to talk about our goals as well as theirs. We share the Soviets' concerns about arms reduction. Arms reduction is at the top of our agenda. No matter what the mood of the Soviets, we have to act in this area according to our long-term principles. Chief among them is that a democratic nation that values human life must go long and far to try to keep the world from blowing itself up.

"But there should be other principles at work as well. One is to bear in mind that a country like ours was not built by self-deceivers or wishful thinkers or people afraid to bear the costs of defending their liberties. The Soviets are now talking about a nuclear-free Europe. But remember that the Soviets enjoy a vast superiority in conventional arms on that continent. The Warsaw Pact has 50 percent more combat divisions than NATO. NATO has less than 20,000 main battle tanks while the Soviets have 32,000. They have 23,000 artillery pieces; the West has only 14,000. And Soviet forces are designed for offense, to conquer and not just to defend.

"The term 'nuclear-free' brings no added safety unless we also correct the conventional arms imbalance and strengthen deterrence in other ways. We must not pretend to ourselves that we can avoid this next round of the arms-control struggle with our adversaries. Admittedly, this is something that concerns me."

Where's the linkage? Why work with the Soviets on INF without calling for progress in other areas?

"We have been doing just that. A second part of our agenda has concerned regional conflicts, those areas of the world from Nicaragua to Afghanistan where U.S. and Soviet interests clash. The particular situations will change, but one thing does not change: The United States is the nation which stands for the ideals—political, economic, and above all freedom—that hold out real hope to the world's developing nations. Overwhelmingly, Third World countries are coming to understand this. In a public competition between our ideas and the Soviets', ours will win. We will not allow the Soviets to upset this legitimate verdict by subversion, propaganda, or military aggression.

"We are not in the business of destabilizing governments. But we are going to help people who resist the imposition of totalitarian regimes. We are going to help the developing world's democracies.

"We want the Soviets at the negotiating table agreeing promptly to a genuine Soviet troop withdrawal from Afghanistan, real Afghan self-determination, and a return of the Afghan refugees to their homeland. We are not going to abandon these people. I've stood there at Khyber Pass and looked down into those valleys. They are a tough people who are hanging on against overwhelming Soviet warmachine technology."

Of course, the big linkage issue is human rights.

"We have seen tremendous oscillation in our stand for human rights over the past years. But when Secretary Shultz was in Moscow for talks about arms reduction, he met with a group of Soviet refuseniks. This particular gathering was made up of Jews who have not been permitted to leave Russia. It could just as well have been a group of Baptists or Pentecostals or any of the other religious faiths that are systematically persecuted by Soviet authorities.

"The Secretary expressed the administration's support, but he also said something even more important: that in recent years, no matter what the subjects of a U.S.-Soviet negotiation, we have consistently brought up the names of the dissidents and demanded progress on human rights. He said, 'We never stop. And if our hopes are disappointed, we keep on. Whether it seems to be a time of hope or a time of disappointment, our effort is always there. We never give up, we never stop trying.'

"In this administration those words have been true. *They must stay true.* Only tough consistency, patience, and a view to the long run are capable of impressing the Soviet Union and inducing its leaders to bargain in seriousness in all areas of our relationship. We can maintain this consistency only if we guarantee that our policy toward the Soviets accurately and steadfastly reflects America's strength, America's hopes, and America's interests."

I remember President Nixon's advice to give the Soviets room. They were supposed to be more reasonable if they weren't pushed on the human-rights issue. President Ford refused to see Alexander Solzhenitsyn when he came to the West. He didn't want to interrupt the private progress in human-rights negotiations with the Soviets.

"Natan Scharansky said to me on four separate occasions, 'Be realistic. Do not be lulled into diplomacy that becomes so quiet that the U.S.A. forgets to speak out loudly on the need for human rights. So many people in prison and in exile are depending on you.' We have to stand for the right and not compromise away our moral advantage.

"An amazing thing happened at the funeral of Soviet leader Brezhnev. Things were run to a military precision; a coldness and hollowness pervaded the ceremony, with marching soldiers, steel helmets, and Marxist rhetoric but no prayers, no comforting hymns, and no mention of God.

"The Soviet leaders took their places on the Kremlin Wall as the Brezhnev family silently escorted the casket around to its final resting place. I happened to be in just the right spot to see Mrs. Brezhnev. She walked up and took one last look at her husband, and there in the cold, gray center of that totalitarian state she traced the sign of the cross over her husband's chest.

"I was stunned. In that simple act, God had broken through the core of the Communist system. It became clear to me that decades, even centuries, of harsh secular rule can never destroy the intuitive faith that is in us all.

"When we went to Poland, Barbara and I attended mass at St. Margaret's Church in Lomianki, just outside Warsaw. St. Margaret's, I was told, is one of 1500 churches being built in Poland by the people's own hands, dramatic evidence of their commitment to their faith.

"What a moving moment that was, hearing the responses of the congregation as they stood packed together, the power and joy of their belief! Seeing in their smiles and tears and the flags they waved how much hope and strength they yet retain, and how their faith endures!

"Everywhere you go in this world, no matter how oppressive the regime, you can find proof of the endurance of faith, continuing evidence that you cannot wipe out by force of law that which makes its home in the human heart.

"Americans are blessed. We have a vibrant faith in God that is our heritage and our strength. And we are blessed with the freedom to worship and speak and to change our government as we please. But we must remember that other people who are oppressed have no voice. If we don't speak out, the world is silent. And that silence in the face of injustice is immoral. Our words give hope to millions."

It's a dangerous world.

"Yes, it's a dangerous world. And one of the most important steps we can make for survival is to recognize just that fact. But I must say that personally I have a lot of hope.

"Several summers ago, at our family's home up in Maine, Barbara was planting a flowering bush that a friend had given us. The instructions were clear: Dig a deep bed, put in mulch and fertilizer, set the plant in carefully with the roots very deep, and then cover with soil and water. If you do this, the instructions said, the plant will not bloom the first year, but it will bloom the next, and the next, and for a hundred years to come.

"As Barbara was there on her hands and knees, she said she realized that she was planting for her children and her grandchildren and her great-grandchildren. In spite of all the problems we face in the years ahead, I don't think Barbara's planting was futile.

"Yes, we have a trade deficit, and yes, the Soviets are in Afghanistan, and yes, the world has the weapons to blow itself up, but something just tells me my great-grandchildren are going to pick those flowers."

Appendix

A Chronology of George Bush

June 12, 1924	Born in Milton, Massachusetts.
June 4, 1942	Graduates from Phillips Academy in Andover, Massachusetts.
June 12, 1942	On his eighteenth birthday enlists in U.S. Navy as Seaman Second Class.
June 1943	Earns wings and is commissioned as youngest commissioned Naval aviator. Is assigned to USS San Jacinto in the Pacific theater.
September 2, 1944	Shot down while on a mission in the Pacific.
January 6, 1945	Marries former Barbara Pierce.
1948	Graduates from Yale, Phi Beta Kappa. Degree in Economics.
1948-50	Supply salesman for Dresser Industries in west Texas and California.
1951	Cofounder of Bush-Overby Oil Development Company.
1953	Cofounder of Zapata Petroleum Corporation.
1954	Cofounder of Zapata Offshore Company, a pioneer in offshore drilling platforms.
1963	Serves as Chairman of Harris County Republican Organization.
1964	Attends the 1964 Republican National Convention as a delegate.
1966	Elected to the U.S. House of Representatives from the Seventh District of Texas.
1968	Re-elected to Congress without opposition.
1971-73	U.S. Ambassador to the United Nations.
1973-74	Chairman of the Republican National Committee.
1974	Appointed Chief of the United States Liaison Office in the People's Republic of China in Beijing.
1976	Appointed Director of Central Intelligence Agency.
July 1980	Selected by Ronald Reagan to be his running mate at the Republican National Convention.
November 4, 1980	Elected Vice President designate of the United States.
January 20, 1981	Sworn in as the 43rd Vice President of the United States.
January 20, 1985	Sworn in to second term.
July 13, 1985	Vice President is named Acting President of the United States for several hours in a historic transfer of authority from President Reagan under the 25th Amendment to the Constitution.
October 12, 1987	In Houston, Texas, announces his candidacy for President of the United States.

The Bush Family Tree

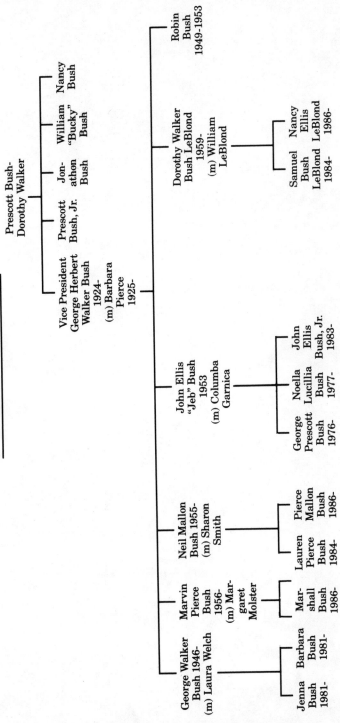

Issues

Abortion

"Abortion is one of the most difficult issues of our time. I have devoted much time and careful thought to this issue over the years. I am opposed to abortion except when the life of the mother is threatened or when there is rape or incest.

"I support a Constitutional amendment that would reverse the Supreme Court's *Roe v. Wade* decision on abortion made in 1973. I also support a human-life amendment with an exception for the life of the mother, rape, or incest. In addition, I oppose the use of federal funds to pay for abortion except when the life of the mother is threatened.

"Frankly, while I have long opposed abortion, there has been an evolution in my thinking on the legal means by which we protect the sanctity of human life. Since the Supreme Court's *Roe v. Wade* decision in 1973, there have been about 18 million abortions in this country. This is a tragedy of shattering proportions. It brings a renewed sense of urgency to adoption of a Constitutional amendment to overturn *Roe v. Wade* and the effort for a human-life amendment."

AIDS

"We must do all we can do to stop the spread of AIDS in this country. We must look for innovative solutions to this staggering problem. The price of caring for victims of the disease is enormous, and it will put an unbearable strain on both public and private financial resources.

(AIDS—continued)

"We must commit the resources and the will to find a cure. American science must know that we have the resolve to beat this disease. I believe that continued research on the virus combined with public education and testing are the best path to curb the spread of AIDS.

"As Vice President, I chair the President's Task Force on Regulatory Relief, and earlier this year we worked with the Food and Drug Administration to accelerate the availability of experimental drugs to AIDS patients. We did this to encourage more research and development on potential AIDS vaccines by the private sector.

"Meanwhile, our government will spend $766 million this year and close to $1 billion next year on AIDS. And as we look into the 1990's we may have to spend even more.

"But money alone won't stop AIDS.

"Those at high risk must be educated on how to avoid contracting the disease. The only guaranteed way to halt the spread of AIDS, given what we know now, is a change of behavior. And those at risk will not change unless they know of the terrible dangers they face.

"I believe that education is primarily a local matter. Parents and the community should control what goes on in their schools. That system has worked well for more than 200 years and I don't want to change it.

"The most important thing we can do is to tell our people the facts about AIDS and what they can do to protect themselves. We've got to put into the hands of parents and students and people throughout America essential facts about AIDS in a thoughtful, sensitive manner.

"The issue of testing raises some difficult and troublesome questions for me. It puts in conflict the need for more information and knowledge to benefit the majority versus our basic Constitutional right to privacy. And it is the responsibility of the political leadership of the country to decide among these competing principles.

"Ultimately, we must protect those who do not have the disease. Thus, we have made the decision that there must be more testing. The government will require testing of prisoners, immigrants, and aliens seeking permanent residence. Tests are being conducted in the military and in the foreign service. Additionally, we are encouraging the states to offer routine testing for those who seek marriage licenses and for those who visit sexually transmitted disease or drug abuse clinics. We are also encouraging states to require routine testing in state and local prisons.

"Of course, any mention of testing must be hurriedly followed by the word "confidentiality." If society feels compelled, in some circumstances, to test its citizens, then it is absolutely imperative that those records are kept appropriately confidential. It is also imperative that help be available to those who test positive. We need testing, but only accompanied by guarantees that everyone is treated fairly."

Balanced Budget

"The most importand action we need to take on the budget deficit is to hold the line on taxing and spending. Raising taxes would only hurt the tremendous economic recovery we have had in our Administration. So the first priority is to hold spending. I support the Gramm-Rudman deficit reduction targets. Our hard work is beginning to show results. The budget deficit will shrink by almost $70 billion from last year's level.

"A President's first priority is to maintain the defense of the country. The question we should ask ourselves is not how much money we should spend, but what is required to be secure. Likewise, our seniors must feel secure in the knowledge that their Social Security will be safe and fiscally sound.

"I support a Constitutional amendment requiring a balanced budget. I support a line-item veto to cut the fat from appropriations bills and put the national interest above the special interests—these are tools that many of our nation's governors already have and the President needs."

Budget

Birth Control –
Parental Consent

"I am against supplying birth control aids to minors without parental consent. As I said to Pope John Paul II, "Our land is built on freedom—but as you have taught, 'Freedom develops best if it keeps to the rules of morality.' We must teach our children the difference between right and wrong, honesty and dishonesty, liberty and license—in our homes and in our churches and in our schools."

"Born Again"

"Well, I've discussed this many times with some of the great religious leaders, especially Billy Graham. I think I would ask for a definition. If by 'born again' one is asking, 'Do you accept Jesus Christ as your personal Savior?' then, I could answer a clear-cut 'Yes'. No hesitancy, no awkwardness.

"But, if one is asking, 'Has there been one single moment, above any others, in which your life has been instantly changed?'— well, I can't say that that has happened. There have been many moments.

"I'm not a great Biblical expert or theologian. I am a believer. I do believe strongly in the Lord and the hereafter, life after death."

Capital Punishment

"I support increased jail sentences for certain criminals, particularly repeat offenders. Unfortunately, there are instances in our society of exceptionally terrible crimes and there must be a credible penalty on the Federal books to respond to these cases. Therefore, I strongly support capital punishment for crimes involving murder, treason, or espionage. The American people overwhelmingly realize that judges sometimes have to impose the death penalty in certain clearly defined and particularly heinous crimes."

Central America

"Five years ago there was only one democratically elected government in Central America, and that was Costa Rica. Today there are democratically elected governments not only there, but in Honduras, El Salvador, Guatemala, and the newly independent Belize as well.

"In Central America, only Nicaragua suspends all civil rights, including freedom of speech and freedom of the press. In Central America, only Nicaragua suppresses all opposition political parties. Only Nicaragua refuses to enter into dialogue with its political opponents. Among current Central American governments, only Nicaragua orders the execution of political dissenters. Only Nicaragua has harassed not only the Catholic Church (and humiliated the Pope when he visited Managua), but has persecuted Pentecostals, Mormons, and Jews. Only Nicaragua today persecutes Indian tribes within its borders. Only Nicaragua receives support from terrorist states and terrorist organizations all over the world. Only Nicaragua provides arms to Communist terrorists in democracies like Colombia, El Salvador, and Costa Rica.

"Only Nicaragua swims against the democratic tide.

"Today, with a relatively small amount of aid to the freedom fighters, we can stop the threat to the region from the Sandinistas and support those struggling for freedom and democracy in Nicaragua. Aid, not American troops, not direct American involvement, just aid. A democratic Nicaragua is indispensable to a peaceful, stable, democratic Central America. That's why giving aid to the freedom fighters is like taking out an insurance policy for freedom and democracy all over the region."

CIA

"As the nation's Chief Intelligence Officer, I saw the reality of Soviet intentions, and how they are cloaked by disinformation and propaganda. That job opened my eyes to the world as it is, not as we might want it to be. The world is complicated, and it is extremely dangerous. We need an intelligence capability that is second to none, and we need the ability to take covert actions to protect our national interests."

Comparable Worth

"We must bring economic growth to the areas of our country and the segments of our population that have not yet participated in this, the longest peacetime expansion in our history. A job is the best anti-poverty program ever invented.

"The American economy has created more than 13.5 million new jobs in the last five years—more than Europe and Japan combined. The Europeans call it 'the American miracle.' The percentage of working-age men and women who are employed is now the highest in our history.

"The Census Bureau reports that women who work full-time earn about 70 percent of what men do. Now, that's up from 62 percent just since 1979—but it's not enough. I have a message for the business leaders of this country: We've had enough excuses. It's time we had equal pay for equal work.

"I am not, however, for a federal mandate to require pay according to a scale of 'comparable worth.' "

Education

"Education is the great lifting mechanism of an egalitarian society. It represents our most proven pathway to a better life. For generation after generation of immigrants—fleeing poverty and persecution in Europe, Asia, and Latin America—the education of their children has been the focus of their lives and the purpose of their personal sacrifice.

(Education—continued)

"The challenge of the past has been to break down the barriers to opportunity. It is a task that is not yet finished. But the challenge of the future is not just to make education more available, but to make it more worthwhile.

"You often hear that you can't teach values. I don't buy that. I think most of us know what constitutes good character. It includes such qualities as decency and fairness, honesty and tolerance, self-discipline and respect for the law. Sadly, not everyone learns these values in their home or church. The schools must play a role, too. We should teach our children what I call the 4 R's—reading, writing, 'rithmetic, and respect.

"I support tuition tax credits. I believe that we should provide greater choice in education to families, and tuition tax credits are one way to achieve that.

"Good education is good policy, and it is good politics. In the years ahead, education can be our most powerful economic program—our most important trade program—our most effective urban program—our best program for producing jobs and bringing people out of poverty. The best investment we can make is in our children.

"H.G. Wells wrote, 'Civilization is a race between education and catastrophe.' We must not let the latter triumph."

Equal Rights Amendment

"I am committed to equal rights for women. I believe that we can and do ensure equal rights for women more effectively through state and federal statutes tailored to meet the specific needs of women—but I do not support the ERA.

"I believe in equal rights for all Americans—including women —and that begins with fundamental economic rights that our Administration worked to provide through economic expansion—the longest peacetime expansion in our history."

Ethics in Government and Business

"It really is disturbing when those in privileged positions fail to uphold the trust that is placed in them. Public service has been hurt by individuals who lacked the judgment or character to put the public's business above their own self-interest. And it's as big a problem on Wall Street as it is in Washington. Those of us in leadership positions in government, and in all walks of life, must make something very clear. Unethical behavior will not be tolerated!

"We need a revival of traditional ethical standards. Despite our national prosperity, many Americans are concerned that we have strayed from our fundamental values. But more red tape is not the answer. You can't legislate ethical behavior. You can lead by example."

Family Values

"I'm pleased by what I would describe as a resurgence, an overdue resurgence, of traditional values. Values that derive from our broad Judeo-Christian heritage. They are not overtly religious. In some cases they could simply be called 'common sense,' or 'what works.'

"You know, we've engaged in a lot of social experimentation over the last 25 years. The truth is that much of it, from permissiveness to promiscuity, from open classrooms to open marriages, just hasn't worked. Much of it was destructive to our family structure.

"Now, let me say that social attitudes will always be much more powerful than government policies. But at the margins, government can act in a positive way to help the family.

"Government can provide leadership from what Teddy Roosevelt called 'The bully pulpit,' and we can do a little more.

"For example, we should provide welfare benefits that keep families together, not split them apart. The current system is a disgrace.

"Secondly, we should enforce the responsibilities that fathers have for the families they create. It is a mockery of justice that

(Family Values—continued)

fathers can avoid making child support payments ordered by the courts. We should go after them hard.

"Family is not a neutral word for me, it's a powerful word, full of emotional resonance. I was part of a strong family growing up, and I have been fortunate to have a strong family grow up around me."

Homosexuals—
Minority Status

"I believe all Americans have fundamental rights guaranteed in our Constitution—rights such as freedom of religion, freedom of speech, and the right to a trial by jury. No one group should have special privileges granted by government."

National Defense—
Strategic Defense Initiative

"Successful research on SDI can lead to an effective defensive shield, one that lifts from the shoulders of mankind the fear of nuclear annihilation. It is both moral and logical to look for a solution that is better than mutually assured destruction. The SDI has strong moral underpinnings. . . . A deterrent strategy based on strategic defenses—coupled with deep reductions in offensive forces—could offer us the most stable and secure environment of all. Isn't it better, as we move forward in the nuclear age, to put weapons at risk, not people? This is the moral underpinning of our program. We are undertaking SDI research and testing as permitted under the ABM Treaty. We are also trying to move our research and testing programs forward so that we can make an informed decision on SDI deployment in the early 1990's.

"We should pursue arms negotiation agreements with the Soviet Union under the four criteria which have been used since the beginning of the Reagan Administration. We are pursuing deep cuts to equal levels with agreements that can be verified and that will enhance stability. These principles have brought us close to success in the INF agreement. In this context, we see SDI as an insurance policy, not a bargaining chip. SDI has helped bring the Soviets back to the bargaining table where they are now negotiating seriously."

NATO and the Defense of Europe

"Four years ago, in an earlier phase of the arms talks now going on in Geneva, I had the job of consulting with our NATO partners on the issues involved. I met with our allied leaders and explained that we had to counter the Soviet monopoly in inter-mediate-range nuclear weapons. Europe and the United States scored a great victory. Four years ago, the Soviet Union was trying to convince NATO to disarm unilaterally. Today, with the Soviet Union facing a unified Western Europe and America, we are negotiating mutual and verifiable arms reductions.

"It all carries an important lesson. Strength and solidarity are the linchpins of our NATO alliance. They are what brought the Soviets to the bargaining table to negotiate seriously.

"Our position on these points is loud and clear. NATO is the cornerstone of our national security policy, of our strategy for peace. We will not allow the Soviets to split the Alliance or to weaken it."

NATO

Pornography

"I support the 1984 Republican Party platform on this issue:

> We will vigorously enforce Constitutional laws to control obscene materials which degrade everyone, particularly women, and depict the exploitation of children.
> We call upon the Federal Communications Commission . . . to strictly enforce the law regarding cable pornography and the abuse of telephone service for obscene purposes."

Religious Freedom – Separation of Church and State

"America was founded as, remains, and will always be a 'nation under God.' The values religion imparts are reflected in our Constitution and in our daily lives, and I believe strongly that morality and ethics must always stand at the center of American society and government. 'One nation under God' belongs in the Pledge of Allegiance. 'In God We Trust' belongs on our currency.

"America is a land of religious pluralism, and this is one of our society's great strengths. We must be tolerant of all religious beliefs. Harsh experience taught our founding fathers that when one religious group obtains control of the political system it sometimes seeks to impose its views on others.

"I believe in the separation of church and state. But although government should remain neutral toward particular religions, it need not remain neutral toward traditional values that Americans support."

Resistance Fighters

"The promotion of freedom and democracy around the world is the bedrock principle of U.S. foreign policy. Market economics, not socialist economics, have been the most successful for economic progress in the developing world. In southern Africa and throughout the world, we will encourage freedom and democracy and the extension of the capitalist system. That is the surest way to ensure peace and prosperity.

"Let me be very specific: I intend to help the freedom fighters of the world fight for freedom. In the hills of Afghanistan—we will help them. In the plains of Africa—we will help them. And in a place called Nicaragua, we will help the Contras win democracy.

"A negotiated political settlement between the Angolan government and UNITA is also the only viable, long-term solution to their ongoing civil war. The Angolan government remains in power only through the presence of Soviet and Cuban troops. The United States will support the UNITA freedom fighters so long as the Angolan government retains foreign troops. The United States calls for the withdrawal of all foreign troops. Reconciliation with democracy is the only viable political solution. The United States supports a democratic government in Angola.

"The United States is successfully encouraging the government of Mozambique to distance itself from Soviet influence. We want them to hasten their pace of reform. We are using diplomacy and other incentives to further this process. We are working toward this goal with our allies who share our overall aims in southern Africa. We encourage an early end to hostilities with the insurgent forces. We believe that a political solution, not a military one, is the answer, and we encourage a dialogue with a view toward a reconciled national unity government, as the Roman Catholic Church has endorsed."

School Prayer

"As a Congressman from Texas, I co-sponsored the 'Prayer in School' Amendment.

"Education is not just the teaching of facts and figures, but also the values that make up our democratic way of life. We must teach values. I believe 'value-free' education does not serve either the student or the society well.

"I favor a voluntary prayer in school as an extension of our commitment to teaching values. I believe that students should have the right, if they wish, for a momentary reflection, meditation, or prayer."

South Africa

"The Republic of South Africa is by far the richest, most powerful, and most highly developed country in sub-Saharan Africa. It is the most influential country in southern Africa—a superpower in the region. South Africa's location at the tip of Africa has great strategic significance, and South Africa has large reserves of minerals which are vitally important to the West.

"But South Africa is a pariah state. The vastly outnumbered Afrikaners, acting out of fear, have constructed the racist system of apartheid to ensure their political and economic supremacy. That system is morally repugnant to all who believe in human liberty, and we cannot rest until apartheid is eliminated from South Africa.

"The United States must balance its strategic interest in a stable, pro-Western South Africa with the equally pressing political and moral imperative to change South Africa's apartheid system. The long-range political interests of the United States will only be served by the elimination of apartheid.

"We need to convince all South Africans—black and white—that the United States seriously desires the end of apartheid. We have taken positive, effective, and tangible steps to achieve this goal. The passage of the 1986 Comprehensive Anti-Apartheid

Act puts in place strong sanctions against South Africa and sets conditions for their removal. Unfortunately, the political and economic effects of the sanctions have been marginal to negative: We believe the South African government has made little progress in dismantling apartheid, and black South Africans have been set back economically.

"In addition, we work closely with the business community to encourage adherence to the Sullivan principles of fair employment practices. These practical programs which build and strengthen the black South African community politically and economically are the key to a peaceful power-sharing in South Africa.

"The 1986 Comprehensive Anti-Apartheid Act is the law of the land and we have faithfully implemented the law. The debate over sanctions was about means, not ends. But sanctions are not a policy in and of themselves. Under present circumstances, I will not recommend further sanctions. Rather, we must continue to use diplomacy and negotiations for constructive change.

"While I believe that U.S. policy in the past seven years has made progress, fresh initiatives should acknowledge new realities and focus clearly on the central issue of political change in South Africa. We should encourage the development of strong, democratic black political institutions to aid in the peaceful transition to majority rule. American trade unions, religious groups, and other groups should work with their South African counterparts to help develop such democratic institutions."

Soviet Jewry

"Let me tell you, I have been to Yad Vashem. And I have been to Auschwitz. I have seen the mounds of human hair, the eyeglasses and toothbrushes and the tiny children's shoes, all that remains of the millions of victims who died there. I have seen the empty canisters of poison gas.

"The lesson of these places is that never again can we remain silent about the abuse of human rights, never again.

"I came away from Auschwitz determined not just to remember the Holocaust, but determined to renew our commitment to human rights around the world. I found myself thinking, 'If we in the United States are not strong enough, not courageous enough to stand up for human rights, who will? Who in God's name will?'

"As Elie Wiesel once said, 'In extreme situations, when human lives and dignity are at stake, neutrality is a sin.'

"Now Mr. Gorbachev has embarked on a policy of *glasnost*, or openness. But openness begins at the borders. I won't be content to see five or six or ten or 20 *refuseniks* released at a time, but thousands, tens of thousands, all those who want to go. And those who want to stay, let them practice their religion in freedom. Let them study Hebrew. Let them pray in their own synagogues. Let them hear the Voice of Israel. Let them lead Jewish lives.

"The human rights issue is now a permanent part of the U. S.-Soviet agenda. It was high on the agenda for the summit. I personally raised it with Mr. Gorbachev. And I can tell you, I will not be satisfied until the promise of Helsinki is a reality.

"Mr. Gorbachev: Let these people go!"

Space Policy

"I would create a National Space Council, chaired by the Vice President and composed of the heads of such departments as Commerce, Defense, State, and Transportation in addition to NASA. You see, our space effort must incorporate elements of not only pure science and exploration, but also national security and economic growth. There needs to be a comprehensive strategy for space.

"NASA should remain the lead agency in exploring the frontiers of space science and technology, from development of a trans-atmospheric vehicle to construction of a space station. What it should not be is a freight service for routine commercial payloads.

"That should be the province of the private sector, and we have already taken first steps in that direction by requiring the use of civilian launch services. But the government procurement process is a model of suffocating bureaucratic excess.

"In the short term, we have to reconstruct the replacement shuttle. But because Mission to Planet Earth would require the ability to launch large payloads, it would justify the building of a heavy-lift launch vehicle, designed for minimum weight.

"Such a vehicle should deliver a pound of payload for a small fraction of the cost on the space shuttle.

"Listen, the Soviets mass-produce such vehicles and launch them routinely. We need them, too. We particularly need them for SDI. Any space-based defense will require a deep reduction in the price of placing cargo in orbit in order to be affordable. Indeed, costs need to be cut by a factor of 10.

"We should make a long-term commitment to manned and unmanned exploration of the solar system. There is much to be done: future exploration of the moon, a mission to Mars, probes of the outer planets. These are worthwhile objectives, and they should not be neglected. They should be pursued in a spirit of both bipartisanship and international teamwork.

"In very basic ways, our exploration of space defines us as a people. It shows our willingness to take great risks for great rewards, to challenge the unknown, to reach beyond ourselves. To strive for knowledge and innovation and growth. Our commitment to leadership in space is symbolic of the role we seek in the world.

(Space Policy—continued)

"With faith in the future and a renewed sense of commitment, we can regain the spirit of Mercury and Apollo. The question for Americans, a people of pioneers, will never be, 'Should we explore the universe?' but 'How can we not?' "

Tax Reform/Tax Increase

"I am opposed to tax increases.

"In the past several years, tax increases have been used to feed Congressional spending, not for true deficit reduction. This should be a warning against tax hikes to all future Presidents—unless you can control Congress's spending, increased revenues will go to increased spending.

"I have recently proposed to reduce the capital gains rate to 15 percent (from the 28 percent scheduled under the Tax Reform Act) on gains held more than one year. We need more investment in order to compete in trade and industry with other nations.

"I strongly supported the 1981 tax cut, which has been the primary engine for the unprecedented strong economic recovery of the past five years. The 1986 Tax Reform Act was a good bill, though imperfect, and I decided on balance to support the final version that emerged from conference committee. As I have noted, some tax incentives for business need to be restored; my capital gains tax proposal would achieve the goal of encouraging risk-taking."

United Nations

"There is a fundamental problem with an organization whose charter gives a nation of half a million people the same single vote in the General Assembly that it gives China, with 1.2 billion people. It is true that resolutions of the General Assembly are not binding in international law. But it is also true that the often outrageous and irrelevant resolutions passed by the General Assembly diminish the U.N.'s overall standing in the court of world opinion.

"Yes, the U.N. had some successes, but they were mainly in the economic and social areas. For example, the World Health Organizations did outstanding work, and the U.N. High Commission on Refugees, despite inefficiency and infighting, saved the lives of millions.

"The U.N. is useful for international discussion, but too often in the last decades it has become a forum for those who disdain democratic values and who seek to undermine. It has sometimes become a forum for the practitioners of terror and violence and for their propaganda.

"Having served in the U.N. and having watched it quite carefully during the last 15 years, I can tell you that the increase in block voting is very damaging. I lament the propagandistic attacks on the United States, I lament the one-sided incessant attacks on the State of Israel. And though I do not fault the Secretary General himself, it is clear that the U.N.'s role as a peacemaker and peacekeeper is minor at best."

U.S. Government Loans
to Marxist Countries

"The only circumstances under which I would favor giving an outright loan to a Marxist country would be a situation in which a government was undertaking clear-cut policies designed to open up its economy to free market forces, thus abandoning Marxist policies for free-market forces that work.

"I believe that a solution to the problem of international trade will come as countries adopt free-market policies to ensure economic growth. It is difficult to imagine that Marxist countries can reduce their debt easily. I find it ironic that Castro has in the past encouraged other debtor countries to default on their loans while he continued to meet his debt payments. He is clearly afraid of changing his system."